THE
ALL-AGE
SERVICE
ANNUAL

Volume Four

15 Bible-based service outlines for those who plan or lead all-age worship

52 sets of 'starter' activities for all ages, tied into the *Light* curriculum, for use at the start or end of a service

Copyright © Scripture Union 2010

ISBN 978 1 84427 519 9

Scripture Union, 207-209 Queensway, Bletchley, MK2 2EB, England
Email:info@scriptureunion.org.uk
Website:www.scriptureunion.org.uk

Scripture Union Australia
Locked Bag 2, Central Coast Business Centre, NSW 2252, Australia
Website:www.scriptureunion.org.au

Scripture Union USA
PO Box 987, Valley Forge, PA 19482, USA
Website:www.scriptureunion.org

British Library Cataloguing-in-Publication Data
A catalogue record for this book is available from the British Library.

Printed by Tien Wah Press, Malaysia
Cover design Kevin Wade
Internal layout Helen Jones

Scripture Union is an international Christian charity working with churches in more than 130 countries, providing resources to bring the good news about Jesus to children, young people and families and encourage them to develop spiritually through the Bible and prayer.

As well as our network of volunteers, staff and associates who run holidays, church-based events and school Christian groups, we produce a wide range of publications and support those who use our resources through training programmes.

CONTENTS

Index of Starter themes and Bible readings....................................4

How the All-Age Service Annual works....................................6

Leading all-age worship....................................7

Part One Service starters

The challenge of following Jesus 12

Hearing from God 16

God is love 20

In God's hands 25

Illustrated letters....................................29

Jonah the runaway....................................32

Jesus challenges us 34

Ruth – God's answer....................................38

Almighty plan 40

Good King David?....................................43

The gift of God's Spirit....................................47

Solomon 49

Living with Jesus 51

Adventures with God 56

Elijah the prophet....................................60

Part Two Service outlines

Harvest gatherers 66

Decision-making....................................70

Jesus for the whole world (Advent) 74

Gifts galore (Nativity) 78

The Lord is my shepherd 82

Have a read of this!....................................86

Accept or reject?....................................90

Ruth – God's answer (Mothering Sunday) 94

Passover for the 21st century (Easter) 98

Come close to God....................................102

Pentecost 106

Peter, this is your life!....................................110

The world's best-seller 114

Miraculous God....................................118

A festival to remember....................................122

Service starter themes

Bible 31, 35, 56

David's early life...25–28

David's later life 43–46

Doing what's right..49, 50

Easter 40–42, 54, 55

Elijah 60–63

Forgiveness 13, 14, 30, 33, 46, 55

Friendship with Jesus...15, 51

God is good...43–46

God keeps his promises 22, 44

God knows us inside out 25

God lives with his people..29, 30, 48

God provides 38, 39

God rescues 40–42

God's love in sending Jesus 21, 24

God's mercy 32, 33

God's power..60-63

Helping others 37, 45

Holy Spirit..47, 48

Jesus..12, 15, 23, 52, 53

Keeping going..62

Knowing God...18, 36

Leadership...16–18

Light for the world 16

Listening to God and obeying him 19

Living God's way..34, 48

Nurtured by God..26

Peter..57–59

Prayer...56–59

Praying for mission partners.......................................29, 59

Preparing for Jesus' return...35

Protected by God 27

Ruth..38, 39

Showing our love for God 29

Solomon...49, 50

Trusting God to answer prayer..16

Service starter Bible readings

Ruth 1–4 .... 38, 39
1 Samuel 1:1 – 2:21 16
1 Samuel 2:22 – 3:21 17
1 Samuel 7:3 – 8:9; 12 18
1 Samuel 15 19

1 Samuel 16:1–13 25
1 Samuel 17:1–18:5 26
1 Samuel 19, 20 27
1 Samuel 24 28

2 Samuel 5-12 43–46

1 Kings 5–8 49
1 Kings 11–13 50
1 Kings 17 60
1 Kings 18 61
1 Kings 19:1–21 62
1 Kings 21:1–19; 22:29–40 63

Psalm 1 50
Psalm 19:8,12,14 54
Psalm 32 46
Psalm 84 49
Psalm 111 63

Isaiah 9:1–7 .... 20, 21
Isaiah 60:1–3 23
Isaiah 61:1,2 12

Ezekiel 37 48

Jonah 1, 2 32
Jonah 3, 4 33

Micah 5:2–5 22

Matthew 1:18–25 21
Matthew 2:1–12 23
Matthew 7:13–29 34
Matthew 21:1–17 40
Matthew 25:1–13 35
Matthew 25:14–30 36
Matthew 25:31–46 37
Matthew 28:1–10 41
Matthew 28:16–20 42

Mark 1:16–20 51
Mark 8:27–30 52
Mark 9:2–13 53
Mark 14:27–31, 66–72 54

Luke 2:1–20 22
Luke 4:16–30 12
Luke 5:17–26 13
Luke 7:36–50 14
Luke 10:38–42 15

John 1:1–18 20
John 3:16 24
John 21:15–19 55

Acts 1,2 .... 47, 48
Acts 8:26–40 56
Acts 9:32–43 57
Acts 10 58
Acts 12:1–19 59

Philippians 2:25–30 29

2 Timothy 1:3–10; 3:14–17 31

Philemon 30

James 4:8a 15

How the All-Age Service Annual works

This book takes the stress out of planning and leading all-age services and, if you are a user of Scripture Union's *Light* curriculum material, enables children's groups to explore the same themes when together in an all-age setting and in their own sessions.

Part One – Starters

In many churches, children and adults share worship times together, at the beginning or at the end of a service. Service leaders often comment on what a challenge it is to offer genuine, relevant and varied all-age content for this part of the service. This book offers 52 sets of four activities to use in the academic year 2010–2011, tied into the *Light* curriculum syllabus. They introduce or reinforce the appropriate *Light* theme. The activities themselves form a rich toolbox of ideas and can be used independently of *Light*. By popular request, this volume provides the starter themes and Bible readings in an index – see previous pages. The starters are also available online for free, along with additional downloadable material – see www.scriptureunion.org.uk/light or www.lightlive.org for further complementary material.

Part Two – Service outlines

Fifteen creative service outlines are provided, to be used throughout the year. Twelve of them complement the Bible material and themes of the *Light* curriculum series, for the academic year 2010–2011, to introduce or expand upon what children have (or will have) explored. A different Bible passage has been used so there is little duplication; however, it would be worth consulting with children's group leaders to ensure that the service and children's sessions dovetail. The outlines can of course be used independently of *Light*. There are also three seasonal service outlines for a nativity service, Mothering Sunday and harvest.

Scripture Union all-age resources:

All-Age Lectionary Services Year A

This imitation-leather book contains 60 all-age services, based upon Year A of the Lectionary – *Common Worship and Revised Common Lectionary*. The flexible outlines provide plenty of ideas for Bible reading, prayer and Bible exploration, all of which complement what is available in *All-Age Service Annuals Volumes 1–4*. For more details see page 127 or www.scriptureunion.org.uk/light.

Top Tips on All-age worship

This 32-page book is full of practical suggestions on running all-age services. It is a must-read for all service leaders. For more details see page 127, or visit www.scriptureunion.org.uk.

We would like to thank the following for their writing contributions:
Starters: Maggie Barfield, Marjory Francis, Victoria Beech, Christine Wright.
Service outlines: Sarah Bingham, Rona Orme, Ruth Wills, Mary Moody, John Grayston, Ali Walton, Victoria Beech, Pam Williams, Janet Berkovic, Sera Rumble, Eric Leese, Maggie Barfield.

Leading all-age worship

Leading all-age worship is a privilege, as leaders introduce God to people of all ages and of various abilities, learning styles, spiritual maturity and backgrounds. In Scripture Union, we believe that the ministry of all-age services is vitally important for the following reasons:

- Children and young people benefit because they experience what it means to be part of God's new community, as everyone contributes, learns and worships together. (Children build relationships with a much wider range of people than would normally be possible in contemporary society. It is easier for them to have a go, make a mistake and try again. Their gifts and skills also help adults grow in their faith. Their opinions and wisdom matter, since God cares for us all as unique individuals. We can all know him and experience his love.)

- Adults benefit as they learn from children and young people, often with a greater variety of approaches than are usually on offer. (All-age services are not an opportunity for Sunday group leaders or people with no responsibility for children to have a Sunday off. Relationships can be developed in additional ways and on different levels from what is possible in adult-oriented services.)

- Visitors or people on the fringe can feel more comfortable because fewer assumptions are made of them. (It should be OK to just sit and watch. Often churches offer an all-age service at festival times that is welcoming to all, free from jargon and appropriate.)

- People with a variety of learning styles and abilities benefit because the interactivity and creativity in evidence in all-age worship require a variety of approaches and responses.

- The team that leads all-age services benefits because the components to a service call for a variety of gifts, encouraging people to take risks, grow in maturity and enjoy being part of a team.

- The church is making a statement about the nature of 'church' – everyone matters, all can know and belong to God, all can be included and all can contribute, whatever their age, ability or spiritual maturity. (All-age services, however messy they may be, are one of the most exciting opportunities for church leaders to nurture faith from any starting point.)

You could describe an all-age service as being one of three different styles of a meal. All have value but which do you find the most satisfying? Which style best suits your church?

Type of meal	What motivates this choice?	How is it consumed?	What's good?	What's not so good?	How to describe?
Soup only	the cook – wants a quick, easy meal	easily digestible	satisfying on a cold day	everyone eats the same whatever their needs or preferences	everything together and comfortable
Buffet meal	the diner – eats whatever takes their fancy	at least one dish for everyone	tasty with variety	not necessarily well-balanced	join in when you want to
3-course meal	the cook – promotes healthy eating, adventurous new dishes	eat in order: starter main course dessert	variety gaurantees nurture	hard work for the cook	balanced and nourishing long-term

- How do you make decisions about what happens in your all-age services?

☐ The time of year

☐ Whatever is easiest

☐ What you have always done

☐ What church members, parents or children's workers want

☐ The gifts and enthusiasm of whoever in the all-age team is available

☐ What the church leadership perceives people need spiritually

☐ The needs of those on the fringe of church

☐ Other

- What are the good things about your all-age services?

☐ Inclusive

☐ Children and young people enjoy them

☐ Provide choice

☐ A Sunday off for Sunday group leaders

☐ Encourage spiritual growth

☐ Reach out to those on the fringe

☐ Enable people to grow their gifts

☐ Other

The service outlines in this book assume that the leaders of all-age services are committed to the spiritual growth of everyone present and that ideally every activity should be relevant, to some degree, for everyone. We have to be honest – this is not always possible, but that at least is the aim.

The congregation is probably made up of people with many differences apart from age, including those with disabilities or poor eyesight, those who find reading a challenge, those with strong views on music, the very young or outsiders. Often, in meeting the needs of one group, you will provide for others. For example, by using a variety of approaches to learning, those with reading difficulties may feel catered for or very young children worshipping with welcoming, trustworthy and joyful adults will be experiencing something of God's love.

A wide range of activities to use with children of all ages is available from www.lightlive.org. This Scripture Union website provides an especially wide range of options for younger children. The *Big Bible Storybook* and the *Tiddlywinks* material, both from SU, are also invaluable resources for this age group.

Key activities in all-age worship

The Bible is central in this material, with suggestions for Bible readings and Bible exploration. The Bible is also used in prayers, statements of faith and calls to worship. All ages can discover that God can speak to them as they read, listen to, learn, reflect on and sing the words of Scripture. The Bible is for all ages! Children, looking for role models, will see in practice how adults value and use the Bible and learn to love God's Word for themselves. To display a Bible reading on screen, or in hard copy, visit www.biblegateway.com to download portions of the whole Bible in a variety of translations.

In prayer we come to God to speak with him, to rejoice in who he is and what he has done, to tell him about the needs of his world and our own personal needs and to be still so we can listen to his voice. Again, as children look for examples to follow, they will see in practice how adults communicate with God, but what is more, they will be able to inspire adults with their trusting and expectant faith! There are usually at least two interactive suggestions per outline.

May God continue to richly bless you in this all-age vital ministry!

All-age editor

Additional material and resources to enhance services are available on the Light part of the Scripture Union website, or www.lightlive.org. These service starters and outlines recognise that some churches are very high-tech, but many are not. We try to be flexible but inevitably we have not provided enough for some people and material that is too sophisticated for others. As with all SU resources, we encourage people to make the material work for their situation.

Top Tips on All-age worship
978 1 84427 125 0

An inspirational look at why all-age worship is not only desirable but doable in your church! Explore some of the features of an all-age church and think about the different components of a worship service and how to use them. Includes practical pointers on issues such as planning, leadership and getting creative.

For more details go to www.scriptureunion.org.uk/shop

PART ONE

All-age service starters

In many churches, people of all ages come together, either just for the beginning or for the end of the service. The reasons for this are varied but include the convenience for parents in collecting their children, or enabling children and young people to experience something of what it means to be in an adult church. But far more than this, it is a regular opportunity for everyone to live out what it means to be a valued member of God's family, worshipping, sharing and learning together, one among a crowd. Getting the timing right is a challenge, for which there is no easy answer! Finding appropriate activities for this part of the service can also be a challenge, which is why the All-age starters are a continuing feature in *The All-Age Service Annual Volume Four.*

Many churches would want adults and children to explore the same themes in their separate groups. These starters go some way towards making that possible, by enabling everyone to encounter the theme of the younger church members' *Light* session during the time when everyone is all together.

This part of the book can be used as follows:
• as a rich toolbox of ideas to use any time when all ages are together in church
• to provide four activities that make a clear link to the material that is being used in any one session in the *Light* curriculum of 2010–2011, either before or after children leave
• to complement the service outlines in Part 2 of this book, with additional material on a series theme (Each set of starters contains theme introduction, suggested songs, prayer activity and an extra idea.)
• each *Light* series theme has a Learn and remember verse which is printed at the beginning of each series of starters. (These could become a feature of your services throughout the year, as everyone seeks to learn and remember God's Word in their heart!)

These starters are also available on the website, as is additional downloadable material, all to be found on www.scriptureunion.org.uk/light – All-Age Service Annual Volume Four. The downloads are numbered in order of appearance: for example, AASA4.Starters_1 or 2.

Each set of starters is linked to a series in *Light* for 2010–2011 and is therefore designed for a specific month. But it is recognised that many churches run their *Light* sessions in months other than the one specified.

Songs from the following songbooks and CDs are suggested. Of course, songs are found in more than one songbook and it would be impossible to refer to every songbook! The following books and CDs are referred to, with their abbreviations in brackets.

Songs of Fellowship (Books 1–4), Kingsway Music (SOF)

kids source, Kevin Mayhew Ltd, 1999 (ks)

kids source 2, world wide worship, 2002 (ks2)

the source, Kevin Mayhew Ltd, 1998 (ts)

Mission Praise, Marshall Pickering, 1990 (MP)

Junior Praise, Marshall Pickering, 1999 (JP)

Carol Praise, HarperCollinsPublishers, 2006 (CP)

Light for everyone CD, Scripture Union, 2005 (LFE)

Bitesize Bible Songs CD, Scripture Union, 2007 (BSBS)

Bitesize Bible Songs 2 CD, Scripture Union, 2008 (BSBS2)

Reach Up! CD, Scripture Union, 2005 (RU)

Big Bible Storybook CD, Scripture Union, 2008 (BBS)

All the Scripture Union songs can be purchased on the appropriate CD from Scripture Union Mail Order, from the website or from all good Christian bookshops. However, the songs can also be purchased as downloads from www.scriptureunion.org.uk/light.

The challenge of following Jesus

This series is designed to challenge our understanding of who Jesus is and what he expects from us.

Learn and remember verse: 'Trust in the Lord with all your heart. Never rely on what you think you know. Remember the Lord in everything you do and he will show you the right way.' Proverbs 3:5,6

The song 'Trust in the Lord' from *Bitesize Bible Songs CD* (SU) puts these words to music and can be downloaded from www.scriptureunion.org.uk

The all-age service outline that is part of this series is 'Harvest gatherers' on page 66, focusing on Luke 10:1–12 and Psalm 67.

Oct – Dec

1

Running thread

Bible reading: Luke 4:16–30; Isaiah 61:1,2
Session aim: To recognise that Jesus was the one predicted in the Old Testament writings

Theme introduction

Ask what sort of books people like reading. Who likes reading about the lives of other people? What about books written about or by celebrities and sports stars? In 2006, a five-volume £5m book deal broke all records. Who might this be? Listen to the start of the first chapter: 'I was nearly called Adrian. That was what my father wanted. A bit posh, I suppose, and it doesn't quite sound like me… In the end, though, my mum talked my dad out of it.'
It is premiership footballer, Wayne Rooney (*Wayne Rooney: My Story*, HarperCollins Publishers).

Try another book: can anyone guess who this book is about?

'The Spirit of the Sovereign Lord is on me, because the Lord has anointed me to proclaim good news to the poor. He has sent me to bind up the brokenhearted, to proclaim freedom for the captives and release from darkness for the prisoners, to proclaim the year of the Lord's favour and the day of vengeance of our God, to comfort all who mourn.'

The words are from Isaiah (61:1,2 TNIV) but who is the 'me' whom the writer is talking about? Listen to the reading of Luke 4:16–30 to find out. Do set this in its context!

Song suggestions

'Who was the man?' *LFE*
'Every day with Jesus' *ks* 47
'Come on, let's go exploring' *ks2* 439
'Take the Bible, live it out' *ks2* 710
'Jesus is the name' *SOF* 870

Prayer idea

People in Jesus' own town did not recognise him, but we know who he is! Set a rhythm by clapping hands, clicking fingers or stamping feet. Repeat these words several times, starting quietly, then building up the volume till the final word is shouted.
God is great,
God is powerful,
God is with us NOW!
(From *A Church for All Ages*, Peter Graystone and Eileen Turner, Scripture Union 1993, op.)

Extra idea

How well do people understand the place of Old Testament prophecies in relation to the rest of the Bible? Show the *SU Bible Timeline* (see following page), pointing out where Isaiah 61 (the Exile) fits in, and Jesus in Luke 4. *Explorer's Guide to the Bible* by John Grayston (SU) introduces the Bible's big story and is great for individual readers, cell and home groups.

Being restored

Bible reading: Luke 5:17–26
Session aim: To realise that Jesus has the authority to forgive sins

Theme introduction

It was the school sports day potato-and-spoon race. Off they went…Then Katie dropped her potato. Johnny stopped and helped her pick it up. Then Craig and Ria dropped their potatoes – and Johnny helped them. At the end of the race, Johnny came last because he had been so busy helping his friends – and he got the loudest cheer! (Or share a similar story.)

Things don't always work out as we expect – but that can be a good thing! In today's Bible story, a group of friends worked hard to get to Jesus – but Jesus did not do quite what they had hoped – or at least, not to begin with…

Song suggestions

'Who was the man?' *LFE*
'God is an awesome God' *LFE*
'Who spoke words' *ks* 387
'My God is so big' *SOF* 1455
'There's no one/Hakuna wakaita saJesu' *SOF* 2063

Prayer idea

Accept God's forgiveness with this responsive prayer:

We've all done wrong things and don't deserve God's love. We have been forgiven.
How great is our God!
We have told God we are sorry. We have been forgiven.
How great is our God!
We have decided to live God's way from now on. We have been forgiven.
How great is our God!
God will forget about all our sins. We have been forgiven.
How great is our God!
He will go on loving us for ever. We have been forgiven.
How great is our God!
He will help us obey him. We have been forgiven.
How great is our God!

We want to become more like Jesus. We have been forgiven.
How great is our God!

(From *A Church for All Ages*, Peter Graystone and Eileen Turner, Scripture Union 1993, op.)

Extra idea

For film versions of the Bible story:
- 'The man lowered through the roof', a short video, using children's drawings – go to www. Max7.org
- 'Jesus heals a man' – words and pictures are from the board book Jesus heals a man (SU) (AASA4.Starters_1)
- 'Jesus heals a paralysed man' from Friends and Heroes episode 35 – www.friendsandheroes.tv

Being thankful

Bible reading: Luke 7:36–50

Session aim: To learn to respond, with thanks to God when he forgives us

Theme introduction

Ask for suggestions for the worst smell in the world. (For example: smelly socks, boiled cabbage, wet dog, the *Rafflesia* or 'corpse flower' from Indonesia.) What about the best smell? (For example: the air after rain, vanilla, fresh coffee, bacon.)

Blindfold three or four volunteers and ask them to sniff some (pleasant) mystery smells, such as: fresh bread, soap, a lemon, toothpaste. Which do your volunteers like best?

The human sense of smell is a bit feeble! We have 5–6 million odour receptors; a rabbit has 100 million; a dog has 220 million. Smells affect how we feel. Pleasant fragrances make us feel good; we prefer smells we can identify; we often have memories linked to smells. Researcher Kate Fox (Social Issues Research Centre) says: 'Beauty is in the nose of the beholder'.

If that is the case, imagine being in a room which is suddenly filled with the most expensive, exotic, delicious perfume…That's what happened one evening when Jesus went for a meal at Simon's house…

Alternatively, tell the contemporary parable of forgiveness (AASA4.Starters_2) originally from *Wordlive*.

Song suggestions

'Who is the man?' *LFE*
'So cool' *RU*
'Jesus, how lovely you are' *SOF* 287
'May the fragrance of Jesus' *SOF* 388
'Jesus, you are so precious' *SOF* 1399
'Your love is amazing' *SOF* 1676

Prayer idea

Burn some incense or use aromatic oils to add a sweet-smelling offering to your words. Lead the following prayer (available as a PowerPoint AASA4.Starters_3), with everyone joining in the lines in bold:

Lord Jesus Christ, we worship you, the Son of God.
There is no other god but you.
Lord Jesus Christ, we worship you, the Son of Man.
There is no other man like you.
No matter how wise anyone is,
You are wiser. For you know everything.
No matter how strong anyone is,
You are stronger, for you are our powerful God.
Perfect man and holy God,
We worship you!

(From *A Church for All Ages*, Peter Graystone and Eileen Turner, Scripture Union 1993, op.)

Extra idea

Ponder: How much are we affected by our sense of smell?
• Wear a distinctive perfume or aftershave and see if anyone can recognise the brand.
• See these news items from August 2009: perfume that smells like cut grass http://newslite.tv/2009/08/25/cut-grass-perfume-destresses-a.html and perfume for Star Trek fans http://www.telegraph.co.uk/news/newstopics/howaboutthat/6094409/Star-Trek-aftershaves-for-science-fiction-fans-who-want-to-smell-good.html

What Jesus wants

Bible reading: Luke 10:38–42; James 4:8a
Session aim: To realise that Jesus longs for people to spend time with him

Theme introduction

Ask everyone to imagine that someone very special (a celebrity, a member of the royal family, a famous sports star) is coming to visit them at home. In groups, discuss what needs to be done before the guest arrives: what needs to be cleaned, what will you wear, what kind of food and drink will you get ready? Now imagine your guest has arrived: how will you entertain them? What will *you* be doing while they are at your house?

Explain that, in today's Bible story, a woman called Martha was busy getting ready for a visit from Jesus. So busy that she was still on the go long after Jesus had arrived…

Song suggestions

'Who was the man?' *LFE*
'All the time' *RU*
'I am so glad' *ks* 119
'Jesus, Jesus here I am' *ks* 204
'We're meeting with Jesus' *ks2* 767
'Be thou my vision' *SOF* 42

Prayer idea

Read James 4:8a: 'Come near to God, and he will come near to you.' (CEV) Play some quiet worship music and encourage everyone to spend time simply listening to God and being with him.

Teach everyone the actions to this active prayer so they can join in, even if they are unable to read the words.

God is with me in the good times, *(thumbs up)*
When I am happy, so is he, *(smile)*
God is with me in the good times, *(thumbs up)*
That's because he cares for me, *(point to self)*
God is with me in the bad times, *(thumbs down)*
When I'm sad he won't let go, *(cross arms over chest)*
God is with me in the bad times, *(thumbs down)*
That's because he loves me so. *(point to self)*

(From *A Church for All Ages*, Peter Graystone and Eileen Turner, Scripture Union 1993, op.)

Extra idea

Many churches choose this date for their 'Bible Sunday'. For relevant resources, visit www.scriptureunion.org.uk/YourChurch/BibleSunday or www.biblesociety.org.uk

Scripture Union publishes books for all ages to help everyone meet God in the Bible. Visit www.scriptureunion.org.uk/shop to see the whole range. For adults, WordLive is available on an i-pod, PC or mobile – www.wordlive.org.

Hearing from God

This series explores how God communicates with people and what he wants from us in return.

Learn and remember verse: 'The Lord is like a strong tower, where the righteous can go and be safe.' Proverbs 18:10

The song 'Strong Tower' from *Bitesize Bible Songs CD* (SU) puts these words to music and can be downloaded from www.scriptureunion.org.uk

The all-age service outline that is part of this series is 'Decision-making' on page 70, focusing on 1 Samuel 9,10 and Acts 16:6–10.

Right focus

Oct – Dec 5

Bible reading: 1 Samuel 1:1 – 2:21
Session aim: To trust God to care for us as we play our part in his big plan

Theme introduction

Before the service, ask several people (if possible, not all adults) to share personal experiences of talking with God. Brief them so that their accounts are concise and appropriate to the all-age setting.

Try to include:
• Someone who asked for something for a long time and God answered their prayer;
• Someone who is still praying about something: do they expect God to answer?
• Someone who had their prayer answered in a way they did not expect.

Set up an area like a chat show studio, with comfy sofas, a low table and a pot plant. Introduce your guests and play soft music as they join you on the sofa. Chat with them informally about praying and bring out the features listed above. Ask each guest if there is a Bible person or story about praying that means a lot to them.

Song suggestions

'God's promises' *LFE*
'God always has time for us' *ks* 70
'I am part of God's plan' *ks* 118
'Pray at all times' *ks* 285
'Give thanks to the Lord' *SOF* 1241
'Our God is a great big God' *SOF* 2004

Prayer idea

Hannah kept on praying until her prayers were answered. Make individual wristbands to wear to remind each person to keep on praying. Give each person three different colour lengths of knitting wool (about 30 cm) and suggest they work in pairs to plait the wool. While they plait, they can be sharing needs for prayer and praying for and with each other.

Then, all together, make a giant plait with ropes or thick cords. Volunteers hold the ends, crossing back and forth to plait the strands. Invite people to call out their prayer requests: each prayer is another twist of the plait. Wear the wool bands and put the rope plait somewhere obvious, as reminders to keep on praying.

Extra idea

As an antidote to Halloween run a 'Light Party' for all ages and advertise it in your community. There are ideas and suggestions in *Celebrations Sorted* 'Star Wars Light Party' (SU).

Focus on 'Jesus the light of the world' (AASA4. Starters_4) by lighting candles and praying together. This would also work as an additional Christmas event.

Listen right, do right

Bible reading: I Samuel 2:22 – 3:21
Session aim: To understand that we need to listen to God and then obey him

Theme introduction

Challenge everyone (or a chosen few, at the front) to play a game where they have to listen and do what you say. Give out pieces of plain paper and crayons. Explain that you will describe a picture that you want everyone to draw. The only catch is that they have to put the paper on the top of their heads and draw by touch, without looking.

The picture is of a mat on the floor. Someone is lying on the mat. There is a tall lampstand with seven lights. There is a window and through the window you can see the moon and stars.

Praise everyone for listening to your instructions and doing what you said. Enjoy showing each other the masterpieces! Can anyone recognise the Bible story from the pictures? The mat is on the floor in the house of God; the lamps burn all day and night; the lamps are looked after by a boy called Samuel (the child who was born in last week's Bible story).

Song suggestions

'God's promises' *LFE*
'Safe in the Father's hands' *ks* 290
'So I'll trust' *ks* 300
'Speak Lord' *ks* 307
'I want to serve' *SOF* 260
'I, the Lord of sea and sky' *SOF* 830

Prayer idea

Many people find it easier to pray and listen if there is something to look at and music playing. For today's theme, an appropriate focus could be a candle or lamp, with dreamy instrumental music playing (consider Debussy).

God loves to speak to us in different ways, so being still and quiet can help us to listen to him. Suggest ways to use the quietness: 'Think about the Bible story… tell God what you are thinking about…'

Play music as a sign of the start of the quiet time and fade it out at the end. Be aware of people's capacity to be quiet: a few contented seconds is better than a long suppressed silence. End with a short spoken prayer or blessing.

Extra idea

Read 'A voice in the night' from *The Strong Tower*, Robert Harrison (SU).

There is an article about listening to God (AASA4.Starters_5), written about young children, but the principles apply to all ages.

Guiding right

Bible reading: 1 Samuel 7:3 – 8:9; 12

Session aim: To see that following leaders who know God will help us know God too

Theme introduction

Tell a personal light-hearted anecdote about a time, probably from your childhood, when you followed or copied someone else – and got into trouble!

Tell a second anecdote about someone in the church who has helped you know God better; perhaps they explained something to you or gave you a book. Ask that person to tell everyone about someone who has helped *them*, and so on. Continue until you have a chain of examples of people in church, and beyond, who have helped each other know God more.

Song suggestions

'God's promises' *LFE*
'Be bold' *ks* 17
'God has a perfect plan for me' *ks* 71
'The blessing of God' *ks* 315
'He is the Lord' *SOF* 755
'We come to be with you' *SOF* 2101

Prayer idea

Explain that you are going to talk with God about other people in our lives. You will all need your fingers to do this!

- Fold your fingers down, so only the little finger is pointing upwards. Talk with God about people who are young, small or weak.
- Hold up the 'ring' finger. Talk to God about people we love.
- Hold up the tall 'middle' finger. Ask God to help people who are in charge of things, such as those who make laws or who keep us safe and well (politicians, police, medical staff and so on).
- Hold up the index finger so it points the way to go, just as parents, carers, teachers and leaders at church point us in the right way – God's way.
- When you spread out your fingers, the thumb points away from the fingers. Pray for people in other countries, mission partners and those living in difficult circumstances.

Conclude by saying, 'God, our best leader, please help each one of us help others to know you.'

Extra idea

Remembrance Sunday

Tell the story of the famous Christmas truce of 1914 when the British and German troops sang carols, played football, shared gifts and drinks – and stopped shooting. (Find details on Wikipedia or in accounts such as *Old Soldiers Never Die* by Frank Richards.)

There are further ideas and suggestions in *Celebrations Sorted* (SU).

Are you a 'leader'? Think about your own role in Reflections on Leadership (AASA4.Starters_6).

Listen and do

Bible reading: 1 Samuel 15
Session aim: To realise how important it is to listen to and obey God

Theme introduction

Explain how to play the classic game 'Simon says'. Choose someone to be 'Simon'. Simon will give commands to everyone else and you must all obey, as long as the command begins 'Simon says'. For example, 'Simon says, clap your hands… Simon says, touch your nose… Stamp your feet…' Anyone who stamped must sit down for the next round but can then play again. Change Simons and play several rounds.

Discuss how the game needs you to listen and obey. You need to do both – and it's not always easy! It's the same with God. We can't obey him unless we have listened and we need to listen and know what it is God wants us to do. (And that's not always easy!)

Song suggestions

'Forever I will live my life' *ks 60*
'Father, I'm willing' *ks2 456*
'I want my life' *ks2 576*
'Lord of the future' *ks2 640*
'Lord, for the years' *SOF 892*
'Trust and obey' (chorus from 'When we walk with the Lord')' *SOF 599*

Prayer idea

Explain this prayer activity and have it in operation all through the service, or just when everyone is together. Give out plenty of paper cut into speech bubbles and thought bubbles, pens and pencils. The thought bubbles are for 'Listening' to the Bible, God and others. The speech bubbles are a visual way of saying 'I will obey what God says' or 'I will follow God's way'. Encourage people to draw or write on a bubble whenever anything said or done in the service prompts them to do so.

Towards the end, invite people to bring their bubbles to a display board and arrange them under the headings 'Listening' and 'Obeying'. Pray together: Dear God, help us to listen to you and do what you say.

Extra idea

The examples of Samuel and Saul show that leaders have a tough role and need God's help. Pray for:

* people who lead groups in your church
* local church leaders
* leaders in the local community
* national church and political leaders
* international church and political leaders

If possible, use photos to focus your prayers. Ask God to help and guide them and for them to think, work and act in God's way.

God is love

This series gives time to wonder that God loves us so much that he became a human being.

> **Learn and remember verse: 'For God loved the world so much that he gave his only Son, so that everyone who believes in him may not die but have eternal life.' John 3:16**

The song 'So much' from Bitesize Bible Songs 2 CD (SU) puts these words to music and can be downloaded from www.scriptureunion.org.uk

The all-age service outline that is part of this series is 'Jesus for the whole world' on page 74, focusing on Isaiah 60:1–3 and John 1:1–18. In addition there is a nativity service on page 78.

Oct – Dec

9 From darkness to light

Bible reading: Isaiah 9:2–7; John 1:1–18
Session aim: To anticipate the extent of God's love in sending Jesus

Theme introduction

Today is the beginning of 'Advent'. The word means 'arrival'. It is the time when we remember that, more than 2,000 years ago, Jesus was born into our world and also that he promised to return one day, in all his glory.

Each time you meet between Advent Sunday and Christmas Day, light the candles on an Advent wreath. Invite a (supervised) young child to light the first candle. Say, 'This first candle is a sign of "hope", like a light shining in a dark place. Today we celebrate the hope Jesus gives us.'

Use the same responsive prayer, (as a PowerPoint AASA4.Starters_7) each time you light the candles. Split into three groups:
Leader: We're lighting this candle as we prepare for the coming of Jesus.
Group 1: Thank you, God, that Jesus came.
Group 2: Thank you, God, that Jesus comes now.
Group 3: Thank you, God, that Jesus will come again!
See *Christmas Wrapped up!* (SU), page 44, for instructions on how to make an Advent wreath.

Song suggestions

'Light for everyone' *LFE*
'Now and forever' *LFE*
'Come on and celebrate' *ks* 34
'Let me tell you about a baby' *ks* 225
'Unto us a child is born' *ks2* 746
'You are the King of Glory' *SOF* 627

Prayer idea

Advent boxes 1
Prepare a set of boxes to use throughout Advent, opening and unpacking one box each week. You will need five boxes that fit into one another, with plenty of space in which to include items, to be unpacked in the following order:
1. a male finger puppet or small-world toy
2. a piece of paper, rolled up like a scroll with words written on it
3. something to symbolise John the Baptist
4. a female finger puppet or small-world character
5. a baby Jesus from a nativity set

On the first Sunday in Advent, invite a child to open the lid of the first box and take out a finger puppet or small-world character. This represents one of God's special people, like Samuel who you have been hearing about recently, who listened to God and did what God said.

Pray that, like Samuel, you will all follow God and continue to be friends with him.

Extra idea

For an unusual way of celebrating Christmas, try an adaptation of the Mexican posada (AASA4. Starters_8) which has been written by Jane Tibbs and used with her permission.

Of royal descent

Bible reading: Matthew 1:18–25; Isaiah 9:1–7
Session aim: To be amazed that God came to live with us

Theme introduction

Each time you meet between Advent Sunday and Christmas Day, light the candles on an Advent wreath. Invite an older person (if possible, the oldest in your congregation) to light the first and second candles. Say, 'The second candle is a sign of "peace", like a light shining in a dark place. Today we are celebrating the peace Jesus gives us.'

Use the short, responsive, rhythmic prayer (AASA4.Starters_7 and page 20) each time you light the candles. See Starter Oct-Dec 9 on the previous page.

Song suggestions

'Light for everyone' *LFE*
'Now and forever' *LFE*
'Christmas Hokey Cokey' *Christmas Wrapped Up!* page 94
'Christmas, it's Christmas' *ks* 26
'Come and join the celebration' *SOF* 688
'Born in the night' *SOF* 1194
'This child' *SOF* 1559
Many more new and refreshed carols can be found in *Carol Praise* HarperCollins *Publishers*.

Prayer idea

Advent boxes 2
On the second Sunday in Advent, open the second Advent box in your set – see previous page. This time the item represents God's messengers, the prophets. Take out a piece of paper, rolled up like a scroll. Unroll it to find these words from the prophet Isaiah written on it: 'A child has been born for us.' Explain that prophets were the people God used to speak to his people. They told God's people how to live God's way. Sometimes God's people got things wrong so the prophets told them how to put things right again. Sometimes God's people lived God's way. Then the prophets helped them see how happy God made them.

Pray, asking God to help you live his way and be happy.

An additional responsive prayer (AASA4. Starters_9) is available.

Extra idea

Make a host of 'Instant angels' from *Christmas Wrapped up!*, page 53. Remember to have lots of (safe) pairs of scissors available.

Go to www.Max7.org for a short video called 'R U Smarter than a Fly? Episode 1: Christmas pudding'.

Find the dramatised reading: 'God with us' in *More Christmas Wrapped Up* (SU), page 59.

These two resource books contain practically everything you need for Christmas time – Advent suggestions, nativity plays, family events and carol services.

Christmas Wrapped up!
978 1 85999 795 6

More Christmas Wrapped up!
978 1 84427 261 7

The praising shepherds

Bible reading: Luke 2:1–20; Micah 5:2–5
Session aim: To praise our promise-keeping God

Theme introduction

Each time you meet between Advent Sunday and Christmas Day, light the candles on an Advent wreath. Invite a boy or young man to light the first, second and third candles today. Say, 'The third candle is a sign of "love", like a light shining in a dark place. Today we are celebrating the love Jesus gives us.'

Use the short, responsive, rhythmic prayer (AASA4.Starters_7 and page 20) each time you light the candles.

Last time, you heard about Jesus being born – so what comes next in the Christmas story? (Shepherds and angels.)

Song suggestions

'Anyone can come to God' *RU*
'Angel's carol' *The Ultimate Collection*, John Rutter, Universal Classics
'What was it like for the shepherds?' *ks* 370
'Hallelu, hallelu, hallelujah' *ks2* 492
'It was on a starry night' *ks2* 571
'Good news, good news' *SOF* 739
'On a dark night' *SOF* 1992

Prayer idea

Advent boxes 3
On the third Sunday in Advent, open your third Advent box to find something about John the Baptist. Explain that John was Jesus' cousin. He got things ready for Jesus by talking to people about him. Look in the box to find something to represent John: a picture of him, or a piece of fur fabric (John wore rough clothing, made of animal skins), a pot of honey or a plastic insect (because John lived on the natural food available in the desert regions).

Pray that God will use each person in the church to help other people meet Jesus.

Extra idea

Go to www.Max7.org for a short video called 'Luke 2 (Christmas)'

The story of the birth of Jesus is one of the 'must-know stories', the ten most iconic Bible stories that have been voted as essential to our culture and which teachers and parents feel must not be lost to the next generation. Read the story aloud from:
The Red Book of Must-Know Stories (SU) (for 5 to 7s); *The 10 Must-Know Stories* (SU) (for 8 to 10s); or *Must-Know Stories* (for adults and young people) or from AASA4.Starters_10.

Royal visit

Bible reading: Matthew 2:1–12; Isaiah 60:1–3
Session aim: To recognise Jesus as God's promised ruler

Theme introduction

Each time you meet between Advent Sunday and Christmas Day, light the candles on an Advent wreath. Invite a girl or young woman to light the first, second, third and fourth candles today. Say, 'The fourth candle is a sign of "joy", like a light shining in a dark place. Today we are celebrating the joy Jesus gives us.'

Use the short, responsive, rhythmic prayer (AASA4.Starters_7 and page 20) each time you light the candles.

Last time, you heard about shepherds and angels – so what comes next in the Christmas story? (The wise men and the star.)

Song suggestions

'Now and forever' *LFE*
'Hallelu, hallelu, hallelujah' *ks2* 492
'Come on and celebrate' *ks* 34
'At this time of giving' *SOF* 33
'The King is among us' *SOF* 532
'King of kings, Majesty' *SOF* 1404

Prayer idea

Advent boxes 4
On the last Sunday in Advent, open the fourth Advent box and find a finger puppet or small-world toy to represent Mary. Thank God that Mary accepted what the angel told her. God wanted her to have a baby boy. The baby would be God's Son.

Pray: 'Help us, Lord, to listen to what you say to us. Help us, like Mary, to do what you ask us to do.'

Extra idea

Enjoy watching the Christmas story (AASA4. Starters_11). The words and pictures are from the board book *The Christmas Bible Storybook*, (SU). (Please check with the leaders of your Bubbles group before using this animation, as it is also suggested in their session outline.)

Go to www.Max7.org for a short video called 'The Wise Men'.

Stage an impromptu nativity play 'Welcome the Baby Jesus', (AASA4.Starters_12).

Find more celebration ideas including a 'True or false quiz' (page 87) in *More Christmas Wrapped Up* (SU).

Happy Birthday Jesus!

Bible reading: John 3:16; Christmas narratives and prophecies
Session aim: To enjoy God's love for us

Theme introduction

Advent officially finished yesterday but bend the rules to light all the candles on your Advent wreath again today. Invite five people of all ages to light the candles. Say, 'The fifth candle is to remind us that Jesus was born. He is the light of the world. When we follow Jesus, we will never walk in darkness. We will have the true light of life that Jesus gives us.'

Say the Advent prayer (page 20) one more time, adding a final line as a shout: Happy Christmas!

Song suggestions

'Now and forever' *LFE*
So much' *BSBS2*
'For God so loved the world' *ks2* 464
'Heaven invites you to a party' *ks2* 496
'O come and join the dance' *ks2* 666
'There's a special feeling' *ks2* 730
'With my whole heart' *SOF* 611

Prayer idea

Advent boxes 5

On Boxing Day, open the final Advent box to discover a figure of baby Jesus (perhaps from a nativity set).
Thank God that he used lots of different people to prepare the way for Jesus. Ask God to use you to show others the way to Jesus.

Extra idea

If you haven't already seen it, enjoy watching the Christmas story (AASA4. Starters_11). The words and pictures are from the board book *The Christmas Bible Storybook*, (SU). (Please check with the leaders of your Bubbles group before using this animation as it is also suggested in their session outline.)

A variation on a popular saying: 'Yesterday is history, the future is a mystery, but today is God's gift and Jesus is our present.'

Go to www.Max7.org for a short video called 'Same again please – Christmas time with Waffle' based on John 3:16.

In God's hands

In this series we hear how God protects David in his early life.

> **Learn and remember verse: 'I have confidence in your strength; you are my refuge, O God.' Psalm 59:9**

The song 'UR my refuge' from *Bitesize Bible Songs* CD (SU) puts these words to music and can be downloaded from www.scriptureunion.org.uk

The all-age service outline that is part of this series is 'The Lord is my shepherd' on page 82, focusing on Psalm 23 and John 10:14–16.

Close to God's heart

Jan – Mar

1

Bible reading: 1 Samuel 16:1–13
Session aim: To hear how God knows how each one of us is uniquely valuable

---

Theme introduction

Ask somebody in church who is well known in some official capacity to stand. Ask one or two people how they know him or her. You want the 'official' answer – eg 'She's my doctor'. Then ask other people. Answers here could include 'She's my wife', '…neighbour', '…sister'. Point out that we don't all look at a person in the same way. Say that God knows us really well and never just looks at the outside but sees the real person underneath.

Song suggestions

'The King of love' *SOF* 533
'When the music fades' *SOF* 1113
'Lord, you have searched me' *RU*
'Even before I speak' *BSBS2*
'Father God, you love me' *ks* 53

Prayer idea

Ask everyone to open their hands flat and touch the finger tips together to make an upside-down heart shape which can then be inverted. Allow a time of silence for people to bring what is on their hearts to God, remembering that he knows all our joys, worries and sorrows.

Give out heart-shaped sticky notes for people to write prayers. These could be displayed on a large cardboard heart.

Extra idea

This meditation (AASA4.Starters_13) reminds us how God sees into our hearts. It could be read by two people or the whole church.

On Monday I go to work or school and meet with colleagues or fellow students.
But you, God, meet up with the real me.
On Tuesday I do my share of the household chores. My family see my grumpiness and bad habits.
But you, God, see and know me as I really am.
On Wednesday I go shopping. Others see me as just another supermarket shopper.
But you, God, know what is on my mind as I do ordinary things.
On Thursday I go on a journey. Other passengers or drivers see me as just another traveller.
But you, God, know whether my mind is on what I am doing.
On Friday I go to the club. I meet up with my mates and we enjoy playing, talking and eating together.
But you, God, are the friend I can talk to absolutely confidentially.
On Saturday I relax with my family. They are the closest people to me.
But they are not as close as you, God.
On Sunday I come to church to worship.
When you look into my heart, God, may you see a person who loves you and wants to do your will!

Larger than life?

Bible reading: 1 Samuel 17:1 – 18:5
Session aim: To see how God watches over David's development

Theme introduction

Demonstrate different ways in which people grow. For example, show a baby's outfit and measure it against a child and then an adult. Or show a simple storybook, pointing out that although it might seem easy, to some it will still be hard to read. Then show a thick book such as *War and peace*. Say that some of us have a long way to go yet as we grow in learning!

There is another way of growing – growing in faith and growing more like God. None of us ever stops growing in this way, and God will never stop helping us to do so.

Song suggestions

'Be bold, be strong' *SOF* 37
'Be thou my vision' *SOF* 42
'Our confidence is in the Lord' *SOF* 452

Prayer idea

Provide small leaf-shaped papers enough for everyone to have a few. Ask everyone to think of ways that God has helped them grow (these can be physical, mental or spiritual) and write these on some of the leaves. Then they should think of people who have helped them to grow and write their names on other leaves.

Display a simple picture of a flower at the top of a sheet of card. Fix a very tall stem to the flower, folded in sections. Ask everyone to fix their leaves on the stem. Lengthen the stem by unfolding it. As more and more leaves are added, so the plant appears to grow.

Finish by thanking God for all the ways he helps us to grow.

Extra idea

Ask people to give a brief, spontaneous testimony of how God has helped them to grow both in the past and more recently.
For a fun activity, during the previous week collect baby pictures from people in the congregation and put them on display today for people to guess who they have grown into.

For more ideas on the early life of David, see *Target challenge* (SU), both the book and the DVD.

Target Challenge book
978 1 84427 314 0

Target Challenge DVD
978 1 84427 315 7

Eight sessions for a midweek club or special event for children aged 5 to 11. Meet David, the shepherd boy, warrior, songwriter and king in this midweek club programme designed to help children meet with God in a more reflective way.

Kept safe

Bible reading: 1 Samuel 19, 20
Session aim: To recognise how God protects his people

Theme introduction

Ask a few people to model different types of protective clothing, such as a cookery apron, cricket pads, a safety helmet or a life jacket. This would be amusing if unlikely people were chosen for each item. Explain that we all need different sorts of protection at different times, but everyone needs God's protection all the time. Thankfully he is always ready to give it to us.

Song suggestions

'Faithful One' *SOF* 89
'Great is thy faithfulness' *SOF* 147
'Lead us, heavenly Father, lead us' *SOF* 321
'The steadfast love of the Lord' *SOF* 549
'So amazing God' *LFE*
'Strong tower' *BSBS*
'Never' *BSBS2*

Prayer idea

Talk about ways that God protects us. Ultimately of course he protects us from sin and death by Jesus' death on the cross, but he protects us in other ways too. For example: from loneliness by providing friends and families, from hunger by providing food, from a sense of isolation by always being close through prayer, and so on.

Give out strips of card (about 15 cm by 2 cm) and pens and ask people individually or in groups to write or draw a simple prayer, either saying thank you for God's protection or asking for protection for someone in a particular situation.

Bring the prayers to the front and stick them to one of the pieces of protective clothing used to introduce the theme. Then lead in prayer:

'Thank you, God, that you are our strong protector. In these prayers we ask you to protect us now and in the future. Amen.'

Extra idea

The Learn and remember verse is Psalm 59:9 – see page 25 (JM1). Check with your children's leaders which version of the Bible to take it from.

Say the verse through once or twice together, then ask each small group to decide how to depict it with actions. Allow a few minutes for practice, then say the verse through again with the actions. One or two groups could demonstrate their actions to everyone else.

Wait for God's time

Bible reading: I Samuel 24
Session aim: To learn how God helps his people make right choices

Theme introduction

People of all ages makes choices all the time, some of which have life-changing consequences, but most do not. Identify a few people who have recently made choices where they needed God to guide them. These could be someone who has recently got married, changed job or moved house. But also include someone who chose to look after or help someone in need when they did not have to, or someone who chose to take on a responsibility in church – try to include a child in this. Ask each of them the following two questions:

What decision did they make (and get as much detail as appropriate)?

How did they talk with God in making the decision?

Pray for all those who have been questioned. This will introduce today's theme.

Song suggestions

'I want to walk with Jesus Christ' *SOF 261*
'O Jesus, I have promised' *SOF 418*
'It's an adventure' *ks 174*
'Love the Lord' *BSBS*
'Listen' *BSBS2*

Prayer idea

Ask everybody to make the shapes with their hands as you say this prayer.

Lord, help us to choose to use our hands in ways that show we love you.
We can clench our fists in anger… or to show our determination to do the right thing.
We can point a finger accusingly… or we can show someone the right way to go.
We can use our fingers to grab greedily… or we can use our fingers to give.
We can open our hand to slap… or we can use it to offer help.
Lord, help us to choose to hold out our hands as an offering to you.
May we realise that we can bring nothing but ourselves.
May we know that we will receive unlimited riches.

Extra idea

In today's Bible story, David did not kill Saul when he had the chance, because he loved God. This was something that seemed completely wrong from the world's point of view. It was tactical madness!

Share together stories of people who did seemingly ridiculous things because they loved God. Other Bible characters could include Noah, Abraham and Philip (Acts 8:26). For modern-day equivalents refer to people like Jackie Pullinger. Ask church members to share: 'the most ridiculous thing I did for God was…'

Illustrated letters

In this series, various passages from Paul's letters illustrate how God lives in the lives of his people.

> *Learn and remember verse: 'My grace is all you need, for my power is greatest when you are weak.' 2 Corinthians 12:9*

The song 'My grace' from *Bitesize Bible Songs 2* CD (SU) puts these words to music and can be downloaded from www.scriptureunion.org.uk

The all-age service outline that is part of this series is 'Have a read of this!' on page 86 based around Philippians 1:12–20 and Ruth 1:1–22.

No place like home

Bible reading: Philippians 2:25–30
Session aim: To see that when God lives with his people they take care of each other

Jan – Mar

5

Theme introduction

Mention some of the ways that people in church care for each other, such as welcoming, helping children or the elderly to find the right page, offering refreshments, providing appropriate teaching and visiting 'shut-ins'. Say that you are sure people can think of many more ways that care is shown. God's people care for others because God lives with his people.

Suggest each row of people plays a version of 'I went to market'. The first person says, 'God lives with us so we [welcome people at the door].' The next person adds to it: 'God lives with us so we [welcome people at the door] and we [give them coffee].' Continue with each person adding a phrase. Suggest saying the sentence together to prevent embarrassment if someone is forgetful. Ask one or two groups to say their completed sentence for the benefit of everyone else.

Song suggestions

'Bind us together' *SOF* 43
'Brother, sister, let me serve you' *SOF* 54
'Praise God for the body' *SOF* 461
'For I'm building a people of power' *ks* 61
'God's home' *BSBS2*

Prayer idea

Display a board with sections: 'need food', 'need care', 'need time' and 'need prayer'.
Ask people to think of those they know, or know of, who need one or more of these things. For instance, homeless people at the Food Stop may need food, Mrs Briggs may be sick and need care, Mr Jones may be lonely and need somebody's time, and the youth leader may have said the young people need prayer as it is exam time.
Give out circular stickers and ask everyone to draw the faces of a few of these people who are particularly on their hearts. Fix the stickers on the relevant sections of the display board.

Pray together: 'Lord God, we bring all these people to you. As a church we want to love and care for each other. Help us to do this in as many ways as we can.'

Extra idea

If the church has a mission partner, it would be appropriate to pray for them in the light of this theme. This would demonstrate the church's care for them and you could also pray for those they care for in their mission activity. Make sure that there are photos and information about them on display so that prayer can be thoughtful and expectant.

Freed to serve

Bible reading: Philemon

Session aim: To discover that when God lives with his people, they forgive and accept each other

Theme introduction

Ask two people to come to the front, who are the complete opposite of each other in how they look, behave and speak, and in their likes and dislikes. Ask the two to make contrasting statements (looking warily towards each other) on subjects such as music, food, clothes and leisure activities.

After a few contrasting remarks, they should mention Christian things such as 'I listen to the Bible on my iPod/I read my Bible every morning,' or 'God answered my prayers, man/When I pray, things happen.' Suddenly they should realise they are agreeing with each other and can accept each other, despite differences, because they both love and serve God.

Point out that as God's people we should accept and forgive each other.

Song suggestions

'A new commandment' *SOF* 22
'Let there be love shared among us' *SOF* 329
'The King is among us' *SOF* 532
'Jesus put this song into our hearts' *ks* 209

Prayer idea

Use two readers, with everyone joining in the response: **Forgive us and help us, Lord.**

Sometimes I say the wrong thing and hurt someone.
Help me to forgive others when they say hurtful things to me. (Response.)
Sometimes I am prejudiced about the way others look or speak.
Help me to forgive others who criticise the way I look or speak. (Response.)
Sometimes I ignore people accidentally or on purpose.
Help me to forgive those who ignore me. (Response.)

Sometimes I get annoyed when I think someone has taken one of my privileges.
Help me to forgive and forget when I feel put out. (Response.)

Extra idea

A dramatic monologue reading of Philemon 1–22 (AASA4.Starters_14) based on the TNIV could be read as an alternative Bible reading. Philemon, wearing vaguely New Testament clothing, enters holding a scroll. He needs to have practised!

Letters to a friend

Bible reading: 2 Timothy 1:3–10; 3:14–17
Session aim: To learn, as Paul writes to Timothy, how important the Bible is to him

Theme introduction

Ask three young people to prepare one Bible verse, probably 2 Timothy 1:7, in different ways – by text, email and in scrawly handwriting on a flip chart or scanned and displayed on a screen. Once they have presented the verse, explain that this may look different but it is the identical verse, the same message from God. The important response is to take it seriously and act on God's Word, however it is delivered.

This is a time to discover, as Paul writes to Timothy, how important the Bible is to him. Introduce both Paul and Timothy.

Song suggestions

'Tell out my soul' *SOF* 520
'Jesus, restore to us again' *SOF* 876
'Lord, for the years' *SOF* 892
'Lord, thy word abideth' *MP* 446
'There is so much to discover' *ks* 327
'Everything' *BSBS*

Prayer idea

Use two readers for this prayer. The first person should hold up a Bible each time.

1 Lord God, in your Word we find true stories.
2 Help us to learn how to grow closer to you, from the example and mistakes of great Bible characters.
1 Lord God, in your Word we find law.
2 Help us to understand and obey the rules that you have given us.
1 Lord God, in your Word we find poetry and songs.
2 Help us to use their words to express our love for you.
1 Lord God, in your Word we find prophecy.
2 Help us to be ready to listen to all that you have to say to us.
1 Lord God, in your Word we find letters.
2 Help us to be grateful for the rich teaching about you and the church.

1 Lord God, in your Word we find the gospel story.
2 Help us to rejoice in your love and to spread the good news to others.

Extra idea

Together, or in smaller groups, write a chatty group letter to God. People of all ages may have several suggestions for each topic.

a How are you going to address God? What adjective might you attach to his name?
b What has God done that makes you want to thank him? Tell God about that.
c What has happened that has made you sad? Tell God about that.
d Everyone then signs the letter.

Jonah the runaway

In this short series, God's goodness and mercy are explored through the story of Jonah.

> *Learn and remember verse: 'Come near to God, and he will come near to you.'*
> *James 4:8*

The song 'Come near' from *Bitesize Bible Songs 2* CD (SU) puts these words to music and can be downloaded from www.scriptureunion.org.uk

There is no all-age service outline to complement the *Light* series.

Jan – Mar

8

Mercy on a city

Bible reading: Jonah 1, 2
Session aim: To discover that our merciful God gives opportunities to be sorry

Theme introduction

Play this form of 'Hangman' to discover the word 'merciful'. Explain that as the children are going to be learning about Jonah the runaway, you are going to draw Jonah running away (not a hangman) and before his last foot touches the ground everyone must guess this word, which is very important in understanding his story.

Draw eight dashes to indicate where the letters will go. People take turns to guess a letter. Either put a correct letter in place or, for each wrong letter, draw part of Jonah running as follows (just using lines and circles): head, body, arm, arm, top of leg to knee, lower leg, foot, top of second leg, lower leg and foot.

In Jonah's story we tend to think it's about what Jonah does, whereas it is actually more about what God does. It is always in his nature to be merciful, forgiving people who are sorry.

Song suggestions

'Dear Lord and Father of mankind' *SOF* 79
'God forgave my sin' *SOF* 129
'Only by grace can we enter' *SOF* 441
'Purify my heart' *SOF* 475
'The price is paid' *SOF* 540
'Love, joy, peace' *LFE*
'Anyone can come to God' *RU*

Prayer idea

Experiment with this before the service. You will need water-based pens, and paper that allows the ink to wash away quite quickly. You may find a shiny paper best or one that is very absorbent.

Provide a small piece of paper for everyone. Suggest that, in a time of quiet, people think about how they have failed God and write a brief prayer or symbol on their paper. This could just be the word 'sorry'. People then come forward to drop their papers into a bowl of water. As they do so, suggest they thank God for his mercy and forgiveness.

Finish with a prayer of gratitude and remind everyone that as the water washed away the writing, so God removes and forgives our sin.

Extra idea

Sand that never dries out and that can be remoulded can be bought at toy shops under the trade name 'Moon Sand'. This can be useful in demonstrating how our lives can be changed when God forgives our sins and they are completely removed.

Mercy on a man

Bible reading: Jonah 3, 4
Session aim: To find out that God's mercy is for everyone who is sorry

Theme introduction

Ask some children in advance to help you remind everyone else of Jonah's story so far (chapters 1 and 2).

Tell the story briefly in a series of sentences:
God told Jonah to go to Nineveh to warn the people of punishment for their sins.
Jonah disobeyed and went the other way in a boat.
A great storm arose.
Jonah admitted he had disobeyed God and the sailors reluctantly threw him overboard.
The storm stopped.
Jonah was swallowed by a big fish.
He prayed to God from inside the fish.
Jonah was thrown up on land, still alive.

During this retelling the children could either create still mimes (tableaux) of the scenes or hold up large pictures they have made. Explain that the story so far shows God's mercy towards Jonah. Today the children will find out how far God's mercy really extends.

Song suggestions

'Behold the darkness' *SOF* 38
'Colours of day' *SOF* 64
'Come let us sing of a wonderful love' *SOF* 72
'Deep love' *LFE*
'I try to do what's good' *RU*
'When you make a mistake' *RU*
'Mercy is falling' *ks* 250

Prayer idea

Provide a globe or map of the world. Talk about places where God's mercy is needed, perhaps showing relevant newspaper headlines.

Thank God together that these places are on his heart too, and pray that the people who live there will know God's mercy and forgiveness.

Extra idea

Use this poem as appropriate in the service.

All you need to say is sorry
For the wrong things you have done.
God is ready to forgive you.
His mercy is for everyone.

Have you ever told a lie,
Made up a story that's not true?
Tell God you are really sorry.
His mercy is for me and you.

Have you ever stolen something
Thinking no one else could see?
God saw, but he's ready to forgive.
His mercy is for you and me.

Have you ever been unkind,
Said something cruel to hurt someone?
God forgives if you are sorry.
His mercy is for everyone.

Repeat verse 1.

(Written by Marjory Francis.)

Jesus challenges us

In this series, Jesus' parables confront us with challenges about how we should live.

Learn and remember verse: 'You are righteous, Lord, and your laws are just. The rules that you have given are completely fair and right.' Psalm 119:137, 138

The song 'You are' from *Bitesize Bible Songs 2* CD (SU) puts these words to music and can be downloaded from www.scriptureunion.org.uk

The all-age service outline that is part of this series is 'Accept or reject?' on page 90, focusing on Matthew 21:33–46 and Isaiah 53:3–6.

Jan – Mar
10

Decisions to make

Bible reading: Matthew 7:13–29
Session aim: To begin choosing to do things God's way

Theme introduction

Quiz somebody on the Highway Code, possibly a young person who is learning to drive. If possible show one or two road signs or a picture of a traffic light.

Follow this light-hearted quiz by pointing out that although the rules and signs are there, drivers still have a choice whether or not to obey them. However, to disobey would obviously be foolish. Similarly, we have the choice whether to do things God's way. We have to decide about the foolishness of ignoring what God says.

Song suggestions

'Make me a channel' *SOF* 381
'Take my life' *SOF* 519
'When we walk with the Lord' *SOF* 599
'Now I belong to Jesus' *ks* 262
'Follow me' *BSBS*

Prayer idea

Be diplomatic when using this prayer! You could use the names of groups in your church rather than age bands.
The prayer today is about choosing to do things God's way. The response after each section is: **We pray that you will choose to do things God's way**.

Ask children under 12 to stand as you say: You are the youngest people at our church and you are discovering new things about the world every day. Sometimes you will have to choose what to do. (Response.)

Ask teenagers to stand as you say: You are our young people and have all your lives before you. You are learning what it is to take responsibility for your own lives in a world that is exciting and challenging. (Response.)

Ask the 20- to 55-year-olds to stand as you say: You are at a time of life when you are at your busiest. You may have to make sudden decisions and sometimes on behalf of others. (Response.)

Ask the over 55s to stand as you say: Now you are older you may be freer of responsibilities and able to choose what you do with your time. (Response.)

Extra idea

Illustrate the parable of the two houses in this way:

Provide two base boards, one firm (wood or hardboard) and one wobbly (cardboard). Ask two people to build a model (of Lego bricks or similar) on the boards.

Demonstrate the importance of a firm foundation by asking two pairs of people to lift the boards carefully, trying not to break the models.

Bridesmaids

Bible passage: Matthew 25:1–13
Session aim: To explore what it means to be ready for Jesus' return

Theme introduction

Announce that you are going to ask some people (prime adults, children and young people in advance) what they know about Jesus. Ask them to say something about the following:

- where Jesus was when the world was created (doing the creating!)
- where Jesus was born on earth
- Jesus' life
- what happened at the end of Jesus' life on earth
- what Jesus is doing now

Say that we know a lot about what Jesus did and how he is with us now, but we tend to forget about Jesus in the future. One day he will return. Are we living in a way that shows we are ready to welcome him?

Song suggestions

'At the name of Jesus' *SOF* 32
'At your feet we fall' *SOF* 34
'Christ triumphant' *SOF* 62
'Lo, he comes with clouds descending' *SOF* 347
'First and last' *BSBS*

Prayer idea

Show a large invitation, ideally one for a wedding, and talk about getting ready to go to such a special event. Lead on to talk about the need to prepare for Jesus' return, even though we don't know when it will be. Ask everyone to quietly talk with God about the ways they need to be getting ready for this. Perhaps people need to put right a broken relationship or own up about something. Perhaps they want to get to know God better before they meet him face to face.

Finish with: 'Lord Jesus, we look forward to your return in glory. Help us to be ready to see you face to face.'

Extra idea

The idea of Jesus' sudden return might be a bit frightening, so focus on the good and glorious aspects by making congregation collages. Give each group a large card background and plenty of colourful and shiny scraps. Ask the groups to read together one of the following: Revelation 1:12–18; 21:10–12; 22:1–5. Each group then uses the materials to illustrate the passage with pictures or symbols. Suggest they keep referring back to the Bible verses for details.

Display the collages as the passages are read aloud.

Talents

Bible reading: Matthew 25:14–30
Session aim: To challenge us to do the best we can for God

Theme introduction

At the beginning of the service give out paper and pens to three people (primed in advance). Say that you want them to draw a particular picture. The first two begin at once; the third looks worried and screws up the paper. Meanwhile continue with the service.

Ask to see the finished pictures. The first should be excellent and the second a good attempt. Congratulate them both. The third person should say (smoothing out the paper), 'I knew it wouldn't be very good so I didn't try. Here's your paper back.'

Express deep disappointment that not everyone took the opportunity to at least have a go. Then ask what we do with the opportunities God gives us.

Song suggestions

'All I once held dear' *SOF 646*
'One more step along the world I go' *SOF 1483*
'The greatest thing in all my life' *SOF 1534*
'God is an awesome God' *LFE*

Prayer idea

Teach the response: **Lord, we thank you. Help us to know you more and more**.

Ask everyone to think of a story or a Bible verse that has helped them to understand what God is like.
Then pray: Lord, we thank you for your Word in the Bible and how it helps us to know you. (Response.)

Ask everyone to think of something in church life that helps them to get to know God better, perhaps the Sunday teaching or a group they belong to.
Then pray: Lord, we thank you that we get to know you by joining with others and worshipping you together. (Response.)

Ask everyone to think of a particular person who has helped them to come closer to God. Then pray: Lord, we thank you for those who have helped us to know you better. Please bless them and bring them closer to you too. (Response.)

Extra idea

Issue a Bible Challenge to encourage everyone to get to know God better: Choose a gospel or passages about a particular character and challenge everyone to come back next week with their thoughts.

Encourage people to read their Bibles regularly using an SU Bible reading guide or WordLive – see page 126.

Challenge everyone to read a psalm a day for a week, choosing a favourite verse each day.

Sheep and goats

Bible reading: Matthew 25:31–46
Session aim: To hear how God calls us to help people in real need

Theme introduction

In small groups, ask people to come up with five good things they could do to help others.

After a couple of minutes, read out a list of people (or show pictures on PowerPoint). The list could include a millionaire, a 'down-and-out', a child, an asylum seeker, a pop star, your next door neighbour. Make sure there are several different 'unimportant' people on the list.

The groups, being honest, put a tick by each of their good things they would do for these people.

Ask if anyone would like to comment on how their group felt about helping the different people. Say that today the children will be thinking about how God feels about it.

Song suggestions

'Beauty for brokenness' *SOF* 664
'Christ's is the world' *SOF* 685
'Give me a heart of compassion' *SOF* 726
'Give me oil in my lamp' *ks* 66
'When I needed a neighbour' *SOF* 1604
'Reach up' *RU*

Prayer idea

You will need twigs or another form of prayer tree, at least one sweet wrapper per person, 'twist ties', and biros or permanent pens.

Ask everyone to think of good things or help that people need. Ideas from the theme introduction can be used. The suggestions should be written on the sweet wrappers and fixed to the tree with the twist ties.

Now you have a tree full of sweet things, you are going to pray for the people who need them. The response between each statement is:
Help us to do good things in your name.

Lord, we pray for those close to us whom we sometimes take for granted. (Response.)

Lord, we pray for those we see in need each day, but we ignore because they seem unimportant. (Response.)
Lord, we pray for those who are out of sight, perhaps sick or in prison, and so out of our minds. (Response.)
Lord, we pray for those in other countries who have problems of famine, floods, war or injustice. (Response.)
Lord, help us to provide sweet things for those who seem unimportant. (Response.)

Extra idea

'Papa Panov' by Leo Tolstoy illustrates beautifully the parable of the sheep and the goats. The story can be found on the Internet. Dramatised versions are available but it could be mimed quite simply as the story is read.

Ruth – God's answer

God's provision is displayed in the life of Ruth.

Learn and remember verse: 'He supplies the needs of those who honour him; he hears their cries and saves them.' Psalm 145:19

The song 'He supplies' from *Bitesize Bible Songs 2* CD (SU) puts these words to music and can be downloaded from www.scriptureunion.org.uk

The all-age service outline (for Mothering Sunday) which is part of this series is 'Ruth – God's answer' on page 94, based on Ruth 1:1–22; 4:9–17 and Isaiah 45:17.

April – June

1

Shoulder to shoulder

Bible reading: Ruth 1
Session aim: To see God provide for Naomi through Ruth

Theme introduction

In advance, collect together a doll or action character plus a series of objects to represent the things the doll 'needs'. For example, a doll's house, a car, some toy food, other dolls or characters to be family and friends, a Bible, something to play music on, a toy animal for a pet, a toy briefcase or apron to represent a job. Hide the collection around the building, keeping the doll or action figure at the front.

Introduce the doll or action figure, giving them a name. Say that to live a good life, there are lots of things that they need. Ask the congregation to take it in turns to call out what these things might be. Write these ideas on a flip chart. When you have a good selection, highlight the 'needs' you have already anticipated and therefore hidden, then invite people to search for them and bring them to the front to build a 'life' around the doll or action figure.

Explain that there are many things we need in life; some are essential to survive, but others are important for us to be healthy and happy. It's good to remember how much God has provided for us.

Prayer activity

In turn, hold up each item from your theme introduction and invite people to say short one-line prayers, thanking God for providing for us.

For example, you could hold up the house, and people could thank God for providing warm, safe homes.

Song suggestions

'All good gifts around us' (the chorus from 'We plough the fields') *SOF* 585
'God is good, we sing and shout it' *SOF* 132
'Give thanks to the Lord, our God and king' *SOF* 1241
'Lord, I come before your throne of grace' *SOF* 894
'Great is thy faithfulness' *SOF* 147
'He supplies' *BSBS2*

Extra idea

Instead of thinking about the things God provides, focus on how God provides through other people. Use pictures of professionals with people calling out what they provide (for example, teachers provide education; physiotherapists provide exercises and therapy to enable our bodies to work). Ask people to chat to those around them, finding out what jobs they do, whether paid or otherwise, and work out what God provides for others through them (for example, mums provide nutrition in the form of packed lunches and other meals; travel agents provide help to go on holiday). Your prayers could then be thanks for the people and the provision God gives through them.

Good harvest

Bible reading: Ruth 2–4
Session aim: To see God provide for Ruth through Boaz

Theme introduction

Explore the theme of being a refugee (as Ruth was), and how many different things they need. Find pictures or video material from sources such as Oxfam, Christian Aid, Tear Fund or World Vision. Play a short video, then ask people to call out some of the needs those people have. If there is anyone in church who has direct links with refugees, interview them.

Song suggestions

'Blessèd be your name' *SOF* 1193
'Lord you've been good to me' *SOF* 1441
'With a prayer' *SOF* 1627
'Faithful God' *SOF* 707
'He supplies' *BSBS2*
'Mighty Saviour' *BSBS2*

Prayer activity

Thank God for all the things he provides for us. Then either use a prayer from the organisation you got information from in the theme introduction, or write a prayer using these repeated lines for everyone to join in after each section:

God our Father, thank you that you provide for us.
Please provide for all those in need today.

Alternatively, invite three groups of people to come to the front and ask each group to identify one of the following:

- people whom God has provided to help and support us
- things that God has provided so we can get on with the business of living
- features in God's creation that enrich our lives, including music and our own creativity

Record their suggestions in some way, then ask one person in each group to lead in prayers of thanks that God provides for us.

Extra idea

Think about what it is like to leave your country (as Ruth did). Ask people what they would miss most if they had to live in another country, doing this on their own or in small groups. Ask them to call out their suggestions. Use their answers to illustrate how much God has provided for us and how much people lose when they move to another country, as Ruth did in the story today. This would naturally lead on to pray for those not living in their home country, for whatever reason.

Almighty plan

God's plan for our salvation, told from John's gospel.

Learn and remember verse: 'He has provided for us a mighty Saviour.' Luke 1:69

The song 'Mighty Saviour' from *Bitesize Bible Songs 2* CD (SU) puts these words to music and can be downloaded from www.scriptureunion.org.uk

The all-age service outline that is part of this series is 'Passover for the 21st century' on page 98, focused on Exodus 12:1–28 and Luke 22:7–20.

April – June

3

PALM SUNDAY

Coming as a servant

Bible reading: Matthew 21:1–17
Session aim: To discover that Jesus knew his death was part of God's plan

Theme introduction

When we want to achieve something, we often make a plan. This helps to deal with any particularly difficult bit of that plan. Ask people what they do when they have a plate of food which contains something they don't really like. Do they eat it first to get it out of the way or save it until last, hoping it won't need eating? Invite someone to talk about a plan they made to achieve something, for example, to learn to ride a bike, to beat the top score on a computer game, to run a marathon or read the whole Bible in a year. Encourage them to talk especially about how they dealt with the difficult parts of their plan.

Explain that God has a rescue plan which we read about in the Bible. This started in Genesis and was a plan to make it possible for everyone who has ever lived to be his friend. You might not have thought that Jesus entering Jerusalem, on a donkey, was part of God's rescue plan. Talk about how you think his disciples viewed it.

Prayer activity

Ask two people in advance to think of something they want to achieve. At least one of these should be something related to the church, such as setting up a new group or a building project. They then identify the following:

- what they want/need/are called to do
- when this needs to be done by
- how they are going to do it
- who is going to be involved

After they have explained this, ask how they know if this is what God wants them to do. Then read Proverbs 3:5,6, and pray for this person/ people in the light of what they have said.

Song suggestions

'Lord I lift your name on high' *SOF 897*
'When I think about the cross' *SOF 2132*
'Trust in the Lord' *BSBS*
'God has a plan' *BSBS*
'Twisting' *LFE*

Extra idea

As this is Palm Sunday you may want to draw attention to how Jesus' entry into Jerusalem was all part of God's plan as predicted in Zechariah 9:9; Psalm 8:2; 118:25,26. This was how we might have expected God as king to arrive in triumph, but then, everything happened quite differently.

EASTER DAY

Dying – and rising in victory

Bible reading: Matthew 28:1–10
Session aim: To rejoice that Jesus is alive!

Theme introduction

Play a game with a Bible Timeline for people to put the pictures and God's big plan in chronological order. You could use the *SU Bible Timeline* or *The Big Bible Storybook Timeline*, (see pages 13 and 126) or create your own. Whichever version you use, work out a way to tell the big story of the Bible focusing on God's plan of salvation.

Invite people to each hold one picture while inviting someone else to move one picture up or down the line until they think they have the right order. Or you could use the following: 'The Bible in 50 words' (by Rev Dana Livesay, Wanganui, New Zealand. Source: *Top of the Morning Book of Incredibly Short Stories*, selected by Brian Edwards, 1997, Tandem Press, Auckland, New Zealand, p41. The copyright source is unknown.)

God made, Adam bit,
Noah arked, Abraham split,
Jacob fooled, Joseph ruled,
Bush talked, Moses balked,
Pharaoh plagued, People walked,
Sea divided, Tablets guided, Promise landed,
Saul freaked, David peeked,
Prophets warned, Jesus born,
God walked, Love talked,
Anger crucified, Hope died,
Love rose, Spirit flamed,
Word spread, God remained.

Song suggestions

'Lord, for the years' *SOF* 892
'Sing a song, sing a joyful song' *ks* 297
'O, what a morning' *ts* 424
'God has a plan' *BSBS*
'Twisting' *LFE*

Prayer activity

In advance, ask a few people of all ages what is the most brilliant thing for them about Jesus dying and coming back to life again. Ask them each to prepare a short prayer in which they thank God for this, once they have shared what their brilliant perception is! You could follow this by doing a fun Mexican wave, cheering a chant such as:
Jesus Christ; he was dead; now he is alive!

Extra idea

If you are developing the specific theme that Jesus overcame death, it would be appropriate to pray for any who are grieving at this time. Obviously this needs to be done sensitively, but it is an appropriate subject for Easter Day. If Holy Communion is part of the service, reflecting on Jesus' death with gratitude is a natural way into this.

Proving beyond doubt

Bible verses: Matthew 28:16–20
Session aim: To explore the evidence that Jesus really came alive

Theme introduction

Invite a confident child to come to the front who announces in a loud voice that they go to '[name of] School'. Say that you are not sure you believe this is true. Ask, 'Where is the evidence that this is the case?' For example, other children, parents, brothers or sisters know the child goes there; they wear the school uniform; they have brought something they were using recently in school; they play in the football/netball team or sing in the choir. All this evidence is presented to you. Now do you believe it is true?

Explain that you are all going to look at the evidence that Jesus came alive, which, when you know it is true, gives you confidence to tell others.

Song suggestions

'Lord I lift your name on high' *SOF* 897
'The greatest day in history' *SOF* 2046
'In the tomb so cold' *SOF* 245
'Go forth and tell' *SOF* 738
'Mighty Saviour' *BSBS2*

Prayer activity

Invite everyone to join in the following emboldened response:
Lord Jesus, make us bold and clear

When we are with our friends and have opportunity to speak about you… (Response.)
When we show your love to someone in need… (Response.)
When we are excited about what you have done for us…(Response.)
This week, may we look out for opportunities to share your good news with others…(Response.)
Amen

Extra idea

In advance, ask three people to each share in one minute what it means for them that Jesus is alive – what difference has it made in their lives? Encourage them to be specific and talk about tangible things. Then ask how they would explain this to someone else who does not know much about Jesus. You could use a minute timer to put pressure on them to be succinct!

Good King David?

God promises David that he will be a powerful ruler and that one of his descendants will always be king.

Learn and remember verse: 'The Lord is good; his love is eternal and his faithfulness lasts for ever.' Psalm 100:5

The song 'The Lord is good' from *Bitesize Bible Songs 2* CD (SU) puts these words to music and can be downloaded from www.scriptureunion.org.uk

The all-age service outline that is part of this series is 'Come close to God' on page 102, focused on Psalm 63; 2 Samuel 15–18; James 4:7,8.

David: a new king

April – June

6

Bible reading: 2 Samuel 5:4–12; 6:1–19
Session aim: To know that God is great and to respond to him with thanks and praise

Theme introduction

Ask two pairs of actors to mime the following:
One person is good and kind and helps someone else. You announce that this person has been very 'good' and kind, because they have acted with compassion.
One person has a choice to do the right thing, such as help someone in need, but they appear to spend a few moments trying to decide. You then announce that they have done the 'good' and right thing.
There are several ways to understand being good. The *Light* series on King David will explore how God is good.

Song suggestions

'God is good' *SOF* 132
'God is so good' *SOF* 733
'Your love is amazing' *SOF* 1676
'How deep the Father's love' *SOF* 780
'The splendour of the King' *SOF* 2065

Prayer activity

Ask people to think of some of the good things in their life and encourage them to call out short prayers of thanks to God for one good thing, after which everyone joins in saying a repetitive phrase such as 'Thank you, Father, for all the good things you give us'. Afterwards, you could reflect on which of these are good and right, or good and kind.

Extra idea

King David was a great king. What can people remember about him? (The children will have spent time discovering him only a few months ago (see pages 16–19 (OD5–8)). Write down words and phrases used to describe David. Then decide which of them are good and kind, which are good and right and which are neither or both!

David: a king for ever

Bible reading: 2 Samuel 7
Session aim: To hear that David thanked God for his promise that one of David's family would always be king

Theme introduction

God has made lots of promises to us in the Bible. Play hangman with what David said to God in 2 Samuel 7:22: 'There is no God but you, as we have heard with our own ears.'
Do this on screen or use a series of pieces of paper for the letter with the dash on one side and the missing letter on the other. Draw the hangman on a flipchart.
This session will look at David doing the good and the right thing – see the previous starter.

Song suggestions

'Faithful One' *SOF* 89
'Give thanks to the Lord' *SOF* 1241
'Our God is an awesome God' *ts* 418
'Praise him you heavens' *SOF* 1501
'God's promises' *LFE*

Prayer activity

Take the following phrases, developed from 2 Samuel 7:22 and pray as follows:

There is no God but you, as we have heard with our own ears.
(*Ask what people have heard about God from other people, then thank God for that.*)

There is no God but you, as we have seen with our own eyes.
(*Ask what people have seen God do for themselves or for other people, then thank God for that.*)

There is no God but you, as we have experienced in our own lives.
(*Ask what people have experienced of God for themselves, then thank God for that.*)

Extra idea

Have a Bible quiz about God's promises, such as:
a To whom did God promise never again to destroy the world with a flood? (Noah)
b To whom did God promise they would have more descendents than there are stars? (Abraham)
c To whom did God promise he would rescue the Israelites from being slaves in Egypt? (Moses)
d To whom did God promise to be with him wherever he went? (Joshua)

David: a good king

Bible reading: 2 Samuel 9
Session aim: To realise that God is kind to us and we can be kind to others

Theme introduction

Remind people of the two sorts of goodness that you thought about in Starter April–June 6. This session you will look at an example of God showing goodness and kindness through David. Introduce the following Bible sword drill featuring the word 'kindness', by asking who was kind to whom, or who receives kindness, in each verse. What does each verse say about kindness?

Genesis 39:21 (Joseph experiences God's kindness while in prison)

Ruth 1:8 (Naomi experiences God's kindness through Ruth) – refer to Starter April–June 1

2 Samuel 9:1 (David shows Mephibosheth God's kindness because of his friendship with Jonathan)

2 Chronicles 32:25 (Hezekiah is proud and does not respond to God's kindness)

Jeremiah 9:24 (God delights in kindness)

Acts 14:17 (God shows kindness by sending rain for crops to grow)

Galatians 5:22 (kindness is a fruit of God's Spirit living in us)

Song suggestions

'I'm special' *SOF* 236
'Great is thy faithfulness' *SOF* 147
'God is good' *SOF* 132
'Your love is amazing' *SOF* 1676
'The Lord is good' *BSBS2*

Prayer activity

Give out a hand-shaped piece of card to everyone and a pen/pencil. Invite people to think of two things that have happened to them this week and record them on both sides of the card:

- one way in which they have shown God's kindness to someone else
- one way in which they have received God's kindness through someone else

In quietness thank God for his kindness and conclude with everyone saying: **Thank you, God, for your kindness to us**.

Extra idea

The Learn and remember verse for this series is: 'The Lord is good / his love is eternal /and his faithfulness lasts for ever.' /Psalm 100:5. Learn this together by splitting the congregation into four, each taking one of the four sections above. Once each group has said their part three times in order, point to each group to say their part out of order. Then see if they can remember the phrase from another group, returning to the correct order. The children ought to already know the verse by heart, by this stage of the series.

David: a king who goes wrong

Bible reading: 2 Samuel 11:1–12:15
Session aim: To discover that, even when God's friends do something wrong, God loves and wants to forgive them

Theme introduction

Give out two different-coloured sticky notes and a pen to everyone. Remind people of the bit of the Lord's Prayer which mentions forgiveness – asking God to forgive us as we forgive others. Invite everyone to use one colour sticky note to represent the thing or things they would like God to forgive them for, and the other to represent the thing or things they are going to forgive others for. Chat about how these two things are linked in the Lord's Prayer then lead people in the Lord's Prayer, saying this line slowly, encouraging everyone to ask God to forgive them and to help them forgive others for the specific things they had thought of.

A prayer activity

Set up one (or a series of, depending on visibility) large, clear vase of water. Drop one effervescence-producing tablet, such as *Alka Seltzer*, into the vase and watch it dissolve. As this happens, people should think about the feelings they have about a person who has done something wrong to them. Remind people that they can ask God to help them forgive this person, so that their bitter or sad feelings dissolve, just as the tablet is dissolving. Allow space for people to talk with God and ask for help to forgive.

Song suggestions

'God forgave my sin in Jesus' name' *MP* 181
'Dear Lord and Father of mankind' *SOF* 79
'Father, we have sinned' *SOF* 1232
'Sorry, Lord' *JP* 463
'There is a Redeemer' *SOF* 544
'Come near to God' *BSBS2*

Extra idea

Use Psalm 32 as a movement prayer. Use a child-friendly version, such as the Contemporary English Version (available for free at biblegateway.com), and invent actions such as the following for each verse. Project the psalm on a screen or get people to repeat the words after you, one verse at a time, doing the actions as a prayer.

For example, they could mime wiping windows for God wiping our sins away in verse 1; mime hiding something for verse 2; mime having floppy arms and legs for verse 3; fan their faces to show the summer heat for verse 4; hold their hands out for confessing sins for verse 5 and mime being swept away by a flood for verse 6.

The story and parable which Nathan told David to shine God's spotlight on David's sin is told in a contemporary version (AASA4.Starters_15).

The gift of God's Spirit

The Holy Spirit brings God's power to the first Christians.

Learn and remember verse: 'Now God's home is with human beings! He will live with them, and they shall be his people.' Revelation 21:3 (part)

The song 'Now God's home' from *Bitesize Bible Songs 2* CD (SU) puts these words to music and can be downloaded from www.scriptureunion.org.uk

The all-age service outline that is part of this series is 'Pentecost' on page 106, focused on Ezekiel 37:1–14; Acts 2:1–21.

Promise made

April – June

10

Bible reading: Acts 1:1–11
Session aim: To discover that Jesus promises to send the Holy Spirit to give power

Theme introduction

Say that Jesus wasn't just a good person who taught people about God. He had power to do amazing things which aren't humanly possible. We call them miracles.

Collect together a selection of items to remind people of some of Jesus' miracles. For example: a bottle of water – water into wine; a thermometer – healing Simon's mother-in-law who had a fever; a tin of tuna – catching a large number of fish; a toy soldier's helmet – healing the centurion's servant; a toy boat – calming the storm; a picture of or a toy guide dog – healing the blind man; a loaf of bread – feeding 5,000; a hearing aid – healing the deaf and mute man; a coin – catching a fish with a coin in its mouth; an unwound bandage – raising Lazarus.

Just as Jesus did amazing things to show people God's power and love, he wanted his friends to demonstrate God's power, which is why he promised to send the Holy Spirit, God himself, to be with them.

Prayer activity

Ask people to think of one really difficult situation where they would like to see God's power at work. Buy a few loaves of bread and pass them round for everyone to take a piece, just as the 5,000 people did when Jesus miraculously fed them with bread and fish. As people eat their piece of bread, they can ask God to show his power in this difficult situation.

Extra idea

Invite someone to share a story about a promise made to them which was kept. Alternatively, ask people for ideas of what promises are hard to keep and why. Finish by talking about how God always keeps his promises, which is why, as we remember the first Pentecost, we can be confident that God will keep his promise of sending the Spirit to his people.

Song suggestions

'There is power in the name of Jesus' *SOF* 545
'More love, more power' *SOF* 392
'Breathe on me breath of God' *SOF* 51
'For I'm building a people of power' *SOF* 111
'God is an awesome God' *LFE*

47

Promise delivered

Bible reading: Acts 2:1–13, 43–47
Session aim: To receive God's power to live as he wants us to

Theme introduction

Invite someone to come a share a short story about a time when they needed God's power to live God's way. Encourage them to keep it specific, jargon-free and under five minutes.

Song suggestions

'Holy Spirit, we welcome you' *SOF* 188
'More love, more power' *SOF* 392
'Spirit of the living God' *SOF* 510
'God's Spirit' *BSBS2*
'God's home' *BSBS2*

Prayer activity

One of the images in the Bible of the Spirit at work is of new life being given to dead bones – see Ezekiel 37:1–14, as used in the all-age service outline 11. Remind people of this, then talk about how these dead bones lay lifeless waiting for life to be poured into them.

Ask people to drop their lower arm so that it hangs lifeless. Pray that we will be ready and waiting for the new life that God, by his Spirit, longs to give us.

Then ask everyone to hold their lower arm bone and wobble it. It is hard but because they can move it, they know it has life. Be quiet for a moment before asking that God, by his Spirit, will pour his life into us to help us to live as he wants us to.

To engage the children more fully, ask them to lie on the floor and feel several of the bones in their body, such as fingers, skull, neck, legs. These could be floppy and then move energetically, as life flows through them. Finally, they can jump up and down and throw their arms and legs around.

Extra idea

The Learn and remember verse for this series is: 'Now God's home is with human beings! He will live with them, and they shall be his people.' Revelation 21:3 (part) Work out some actions or signs for this verse and use them as you learn the verse together. The signs will indicate how much everyone understands what this means. You could split into small groups with each group then demonstrating their actions for the benefit of others.

Solomon

Solomon displays the importance of honouring God and reflecting his holiness.

Learn and remember verse **'They were calling out to each other: "Holy, holy, holy! The Lord Almighty is holy! His glory fills the world."'** Isaiah 6:3

The song 'Holy' from *Bitesize Bible Songs 2* CD (SU) puts these words to music and can be downloaded from www.scriptureunion.org.uk

There is no all-age service outline to link with the two sessions in this series.

God moves in

Bible reading: 1 Kings 5–8; Psalm 84
Session aim: To realise that how we do things is important to God

April – June

12

Theme introduction

Write some activities and some adverbs each on separate pieces of paper or card and place them inside two bags. Ask volunteers to pick one card from each bag and then to mime the activity in the manner of the adverb. This should be a fun activity. Challenge people to guess both the activity and the adverb (the manner in which the activity is being done).

Examples of activities might be: putting out the washing, building a brick tower, going in a lift, riding a bike or getting dressed.

Examples of adverbs might be: slowly, fast, crazily, sleepily, seriously, happily, sadly, gently or roughly.

Explain that when we look at how to live God's way, it's not just important *what* we do but also *how* we do it.

Song suggestions

'Be bold, be strong' *SOF* 37
'Be thou my vision' *SOF* 42
'He who would valiant be' *SOF* 174
'Everyone needs compassion' *SOF* 1757

Prayer activity

So, when it comes to praying, it's just as important *how* we pray as *what* we pray. Ask for some words to describe good ways to pray, for example: simply, honestly, humbly.
Implement these in how you lead in prayer at the start of the service, including asking God to help you to pray in the way he wants.

Extra idea

Lead a Bible quiz where teams have multiple choice questions to answer about how people did various activities.

For example (the first adverb in the list below is the answer, so change the order when you present the choices):

Abraham obeyed faithfully / slowly / reluctantly / eventually
Jonah went to Nineveh reluctantly / faithfully / boldly / swiftly
The disciples spoke God's message bravely / quietly / loudly / slowly
The Corinthians gave their money generously / rashly / reluctantly / meanly

Solomon moves out

Bible readings: I Kings 11:1–13;26–43;12:1 – 13:10; Psalm 1
Session aim: To remember that there are consequences if we ignore God

Theme introduction

Give some examples of times when we might be tempted to ignore someone, or ask for ideas of what might happen if we ignore good advice.

For example: we ignore our parent's advice; we ignore the lollipop lady who tells us to wait before crossing the road; we ignore the letter from the DVLA to say our car tax is about to expire; we ignore our friend telling us when their birthday is.

There are always consequences to ignoring someone, sometimes good, sometimes bad, but always bad when we ignore God. King Solomon was to find this out!

Song suggestions

'When we walk with the Lord' SOF 599
'The wise man built' JP 252
'The Lord's my shepherd' SOF 1030
'Lord I come to you' SOF 895
'Faithful One' SOF 89

Prayer activity

Explain that sometimes we ignore God on purpose, but at other times we just forget to remember him. Pass around boxes of beads and 15 cm pieces of embroidery thread, encouraging everyone to take one of each. You could give these out as people arrive. Encourage everyone to make a plan of somewhere to tie their bead and thread to remind them to remember God. They could tie it around their wrist, attach it to a bag or purse, put it in a pocket or wallet, tie it to their bed or fix it to the fridge door. Encourage people to be creative in their plans.

Everyone then holds their bead in their hand while you ask God to help you not to forget or ignore him.

Extra idea

Psalm 1 is a great reminder of the difference between those who delight in God and the wicked. Everyone could read it in two halves, using a displayed version or printed on the notice sheet or from church Bibles. The 'blessed' read verses 1-3, 6a, while the 'wicked' read verses 4,5,6b. In advance, children could work out some dramatic actions and sound effects such as water and wind effects, a menacing gong, laughter, miserable sighing.

Everyone could say verse 6a several times at the end.

Living with Jesus

Explore Peter's experience of God's goodness and mercy as he follows Jesus.

Learn and remember verse: 'Come back to the Lord your God. He is kind and full of mercy; he is patient and keeps his promise; he is always ready to forgive and not punish.' Joel 2:13b

The song 'Come back' from *Bitesize Bible Songs* CD (SU) puts these words to music and can be downloaded from www.scriptureunion.org.uk

The all-age service outline that is part of this series is 'Peter, this is your life!' on page 110, focused on Mark 1:16–20; John 21:15–19 and Joel 2:12,13.

New way of life

July – Sept 1

Bible reading: Mark 1:16–20
Session aim: To discover that Jesus wants people to follow him

Theme introduction

Ask for volunteers to learn some dance steps. (If you are not a dancer, find someone else to lead this or teach another skill where the learner has to 'follow' the teacher.) Make sure you use the word 'follow' as you ask the volunteers to watch and copy what you do.

Explain that it can be fun teaching people new things. Ask the volunteers what they had to do to follow what you were teaching them. Draw out that they needed to listen and watch carefully, trying to copy what you did and how you did it.

Jesus wants people to follow him, and when we are called to be his followers, we will be learning something more valuable than a few dance steps. Our lives will change for the better as we learn from him. This happened to Peter (or Simon as he was originally called). His story will be told over the next few weeks.

Song suggestions

'Will you come and follow me?' *SOF* 1120
'Jesus is greater than the greatest heroes' *ts* 282
'Jesus, take me as I am' *SOF* 305
'Jesus, all for Jesus' *SOF* 1376
'I have decided to follow Jesus' *JP* 98
'Come back' *BSBS*

Prayer idea

Divide the congregation into two halves. One half will say the words of Jesus recorded in Mark 1:17: 'Come with me!' or 'Follow me!' and the other half should respond by saying, 'We will come with you/follow you, Jesus', standing up to signal their willingness to follow. Then reverse the roles so that the first half also has a chance to respond to Jesus' call.

This could be followed by a short time for people to think of two places or ways in which they will follow Jesus this week and for them to talk with him about this. Conclude by saying together, 'We will come with you/follow you, Jesus'.

Extra idea

Use the hymn 'Will you come and follow me?' (selecting verses which seem appropriate to your congregation). All but the last verse could be sung or said by one person (or a small group) to illustrate that these represent the call of Jesus. Everyone could sing the final verse, 'Lord, your summons echoes true...' as a response. Include the youngest children by leading them around the room playing 'follow my leader' during the singing.

New understanding

Bible reading: Mark 8:27–30

Session aim: To explore how Jesus helps us know who he is

Theme introduction

Choose an identity (perhaps a famous person, Bible character or local personality). Play 'Who am I?' Explain that you are pretending to be someone in particular and invite people to ask questions to find out who you are. You will only answer 'yes' or 'no', but you can give extra clues from time to time. Play this game a couple of times, perhaps with someone else taking on a mystery identity.

Discuss how people found out who you were pretending to be, drawing out that they needed to ask questions and listen to the answers and to each other; you helped by answering questions and providing clues.

Conclude that Jesus wants us to know who he is. You could challenge everyone, in small groups, to think of ways in which Jesus does this. Suggest that the game just played might help them.

Song suggestions

'Jesus is the name we honour' *ts* 285
'More about Jesus would I know' *ts* 358
'Jesus, my Lord' *MP* 374
'Jesus, Jesus, holy and anointed One' *SOF* 293
'Jesus, Jesus, Healer, Saviour' *SOF* 1388
'You are the King of glory' *JP* 296

Prayer idea

Say the following prayer, using the actions if younger children are present:

Jesus, we're here today to find out more about who you are.
Help us listen well. (*Cup ear with hand.*)
Help us use our eyes for clues. (*Point to eyes.*)
Help us ask the right questions. (*Point to mouth.*)
Help us to think carefully. (*Point to head.*)
So that we'll know you better and love you more.
Amen

Extra idea

Give out pieces of coloured paper on which people can write something they have found out about Jesus using the formula 'Jesus is...' Ask for just one or two words to be added. After the service make a poster, arranging the pieces of paper to form the word MESSIAH, which is what Peter had found out about Jesus (Mark 8:29). Display the poster in a prominent place for the remainder of this series.

New perspective

Bible reading: Mark 9:2–13
Session aim: To find out that Jesus is extraordinary

Theme introduction

Tell the stories of some extraordinary people, such as one of the following:

Oscar Pistorius was born with a rare condition that meant both of his legs had to be amputated. With the help of state-of-the-art artificial legs, he has become one of the fastest runners in the world, capable even of beating able-bodied athletes.

Akrit Jaswal, a seven-year-old Indian boy operated on a young girl in India who had been badly burnt, her fingers had fused together and curled into a knotted ball. The operation was a success.

Marc Yu is a young pianist. At seven years old he could play more than forty classical pieces from memory.

Every person has something amazing about them, but some are so extraordinary that we can scarcely believe the things they are able to do. In some ways, Jesus was just another human being, but in other ways he was extraordinary. The Jewish people were looking for a super-hero, whom they called 'The Messiah', to come and help them. What might have happened to make Peter say to Jesus, 'You are the Messiah'? Invite comments.

Song suggestions

'All heaven declares' *ts* 8
'Shout for joy and sing' *ts* 450
'Jesus, name above all names' *SOF* 298
'Majesty' *SOF* 379
'Lord Jesus, robed in splendour' *SOF* 1429
'Jesus, how lovely you are' *JP* 133

Prayer idea

Take the word 'extraordinary' and invite people to say words that mean something similar. Choosing four or five of these words that might apply to Jesus, ask different sections of the congregation to remember one each. Then lead the following prayer:

Healing and teaching, Jesus you are... (*point to one section so that they say their 'extraordinary' word*).
Caring and challenging, Jesus you are... (*next section*).
Guide and goal, Jesus you are... (*next section*).
Example and friend, Jesus you are... (*next section*).
Dying and rising, Jesus you are... (*next section*).

Extra idea

Interview someone who has achieved something extraordinary and draw out the extent to which Jesus has been an inspiration for him or her.

Old fears

Bible reading: Mark 14:27–31,66–72

Session aim: To realise that Jesus' friends sometimes got it wrong

Theme introduction

Ask the congregation to imagine that they are a world-class athlete. Go through the preparation needed for a major event – the training, the attention to diet and lifestyle and so on. Then invite them to imagine the event has come, the race is reaching a climax, only a few more metres to go and you are in the lead; you are reaching for the finishing line and... you stumble and fall! How do you feel? After all that preparation, training and hope you make a mistake and it's all over!

Perhaps this gives us some idea how Peter felt when, after years of following Jesus and making grand promises that he would never let him down, he got it wrong. He wanted to stand by Jesus to the end, but in a single moment, his courage failed.

Even the closest followers of Jesus can sometimes get it wrong. (You may even like to admit that you sometimes get it wrong!) But what does an athlete do if he or she trips and loses the chance of winning? Point out that we can always get up and keep going. Friends of Jesus don't have to do this alone; they can do this with his help. You could refer back to Starter AJ9, page 46.

Song suggestions

'Dear Lord and Father' *ts* 79
'I believe in Jesus' *ts* 195
'You are merciful to me' *ts* 593
'Father, we have sinned' *SOF* 1232
'I come as I am' *SOF* 1303
'All you have to do' *JP* 307
'Sorry, Lord' *JP* 463

Prayer idea

In advance, download or make a recording of a cock (or rooster) crowing. (This should be easily accessible with an online search.) Copy the words of Psalm 19:8,12,14 onto your service sheet or display them clearly. Remind everyone that when Peter got it wrong, he heard a cock crowing. Encourage everyone to listen out for this sound. First let everyone read verse 8. Leave a pause then play the recording. Follow this by reading verse 12 together. Again leave a pause before playing the recording. Conclude with everyone reading verse 14.

Extra idea

Play this game (which most people will get wrong). Mark up some large cards with the numbers 1 to 10. Ask a volunteer to shuffle the cards and hold one up at random. You should then ask, 'How many?' The answer is not the number on the card, but the number of fingers you hold up as you ask. (Don't make this too obvious at first.) Repeat the game until someone gets it right!

New start

Bible reading: John 21:15–19
Session aim: To discover that Jesus welcomes us back

Theme introduction

Arrange for a small group to mime (no words) the action from Jesus' parable of the loving father (Luke 15:11–32), challenging the rest of the congregation to guess this well known story. Afterwards, draw parallels between the parable and today's Bible reading. In the parable the son let his father down badly, but the father was overjoyed when he returned and restored him to his place in the family. Jesus restored Peter even though he had failed him at his time of need.

Make the point that Jesus taught people that God welcomes us back when we have done things which are wrong. Not only that, he put his teaching into practice! Jesus hasn't changed. He welcomed Peter back and he will welcome us back too.

Song suggestions

'I'm special' *ts* 222
'You loved me as you found me' *ts* 602
'Lord of every heart' *SOF* 1432
'Once I was far away' *SOF* 1482
'God is good' *JP* 55
'I was lost but Jesus found me' *JP* 125

Prayer idea

Invite everyone to listen to the following and respond in silence to the question at the end.

Who is welcome here?
The liars, the cheats, the cynics, the bullies;
The thieves, the gossips, the proud;
Cowards and drifters, the lazy, the ruthless;
Those going along with the crowd.
Swindlers and doubters, the selfish, the cruel;
The greedy, the bitter, the vain;
Those who couldn't care less, those who don't even try
Or make errors again and again.
All are welcomed by Jesus; he wants us to come;
He calls us to come and be free.
But the question he asks us will change what we are.
Jesus asks us, 'Now, do you love me?'

Extra idea

Give an extra welcome this week at the beginning of the service. You could pass round chocolates, distribute flowers or bookmarks or simply encourage people to talk with one another, especially those they do not know well, perhaps to ask for any news or special concerns they have.

Adventures with God

A series about our God who communicates.

Learn and remember verse: 'Everything in the Scriptures is God's Word. All of it is useful for teaching and helping people and for correcting them and showing them how to live.' 2 Timothy 3:16 (CEV)

The song 'Everything' from *Bitesize Bible Songs* CD (SU) puts these words to music and can be downloaded from www.scriptureunion.org.uk

The all-age service outline that is part of this series is 'The world's best-seller', a service outline on the Bible, on page 114, based on Psalm 119:97–105,127 and 2 Timothy 3:16.

July – Sept
6

Philip explains

Bible reading: Acts 8:26–40
Session aim: To discover that God speaks through his Word

Theme introduction

Ask how many people present know their parents' names – the majority will. Ask about grandparents and great-grandparents. (Younger children could be invited to draw their families and show the pictures later.) Discuss how one would find out about family members who lived long ago (from older people who knew them, from records in libraries or on the Internet and so on). If you have time, interview someone who has discovered something interesting through family research.

Explain that written records are a good source of information and introduce the Bible as a written record which helps us discover more about God. It contains the writings and stories of many people who were on adventures with God, like Philip whose story is today's Bible passage.

When we read or hear this written record, something amazing happens. We find ourselves on an adventure with God too! And God can speak to us, just as he has spoken to people all through the ages. The Bible is sometimes referred to as God's Word for that very reason. God speaks through his Word. The more we read the Bible, the more we listen, the more we try to understand it (which is not always easy), the further we travel on our adventure with God.

Song suggestions

'Lord, for the years' *ts* 327
'Thy word' *SOF* 1066
'Be still and know that I am God' *JP* 22
'Father, your word' *JP* 338
'Now in reverence and awe' *SOF* 1468
'Everything' *BSBS* CD

Prayer idea

Show a PowerPoint presentation which combines words from the Bible with suitable background images, adding soft music if you wish. Since children will be present, the words should also be read aloud. Invite the congregation to pay attention to the words, so that God might speak through his Word as they hear it. Psalm 1 is suitable and is available as a download (AASA4.Starters_16).

Extra idea

Encourage personal Bible reading by creating a display of Bible guides for various ages. You could offer these on a 'buy or return' basis. Arrange for someone to be on hand to explain how to use the different kinds of guides. For details of Scripture Union's resources visit www.scriptureunion.org.uk or www.wordlive.org.

Peter prays

Bible reading: Acts 9:32–43

Session aim: To discover that God acts when people pray

Theme introduction

Prepare slips of paper with statements such as:
'I prayed to become rich.'
'I prayed that someone who hurt me would get hurt too.'
'I prayed that I would be allowed to have lots of sweets.'
'I prayed that I would be the best footballer in the world.'

Add some positive examples such as:
'I prayed that my friend would get well.'
'I prayed for a chance to tell others about Jesus.'
'I prayed for a friend in trouble to be strong.'

Ask for volunteers to read these out in random order. Together decide which prayers are likely to be answered and arrange the readers into two groups accordingly. Point out that when on our adventure with God, it is important to pray as Peter did on his adventure with God. God did amazing things as a result of Peter's prayers. God acts when we pray, although we do not know how he will act. But we do know that God will act in some way when our prayers are for good, loving, unselfish things to happen.

Prayer idea

Make seven large cards, each with one letter (G-O-D - A-C-T-S) written on it. Leave these around the room with a few pens and crayons beside each one. Ask everyone to think of things they would like to pray for and to draw or write them in two or three words on the back of one of the cards. Encourage a prayerful atmosphere during this activity. When this is done, ask seven volunteers to bring a card forward and stand in the correct order, holding the cards down. Pray, 'Thank you, God, for hearing our prayers.' The cards should be lifted and the congregation responds by saying, 'God acts!'

Extra idea

Ask everyone to listen to an account of Peter's adventure with God as today's Bible story is read. They should listen out for the prayers that Peter prayed and note how God acted. You could organise a small group to mime the action of the story, making sure that the mime is rehearsed with the Bible reader.

Song suggestions

'Father, hear our prayer' *ts* 93
'Holy Spirit, come' *ts* 180
'Make me a channel' *ts* 348
'What a friend we have in Jesus' *JP* 273
'Bring your best to their worst' *SOF* 1196

Cornelius prays

Bible reading: Acts 10
Session aim: To discover that God speaks in unexpected ways

Theme introduction

We might expect God to speak through his Word, through nature or through other Christian people, but the following experimental activity suggests that God sometimes speaks through unexpected ways. It needs to be introduced carefully.

Show a large sheet or a sail and explain how on Peter's adventure with God, he had a dream or vision of a sheet being lowered by its four corners to the earth. Get four (tall) volunteers to demonstrate this. Peter found that God had given him this vision because he had a special message for him. God had spoken in an unexpected way.

Read Acts 10:9–16 to find out the meaning of the vision. Comment that Peter's concerns at that time are not necessarily ours, but God wants to speak to us about things that concern us. Invite everyone to watch the sheet being lowered and lifted three times, asking them to be open to anything God wants to say to them.

Afterwards, reassure the congregation that this may not have been the right time for God to speak to everyone, but challenge them to be open to unexpected encounters with God in the days ahead.

Song suggestions

'Father, I place into your hands' *ts* 97
'As we seek your face' *ts* 31
'At your feet, O Lord' *MP* 44
'Let God speak' *SOF* 324
'The voice of God' *SOF* 1556

Prayer idea

Can you find someone who can give a short personal testimony about how God has spoken to them in an unusual situation, such as on holiday, the birth of a child, walking down the street thinking of nothing much, in a dream? This would be an appropriate time to talk about how you discern whether or not it is the voice of God. Look at the story of Peter and Cornelius again. How could Peter be sure that this was God's Word to him?

Extra idea

Today's Bible passage is very long and repetitive, so divide the reading as follows between two readers, one to represent Peter and the other Cornelius:
Verses 1–8: Cornelius
9–23: Peter
24: Cornelius
25–27,34,35: Peter
44,45: Cornelius
46–48: Peter

Peter escapes

Bible reading: Acts 12:1–19
Session aim: To discover that God responds when his people pray

Theme introduction

Show a device or gadget that responds in an interesting or surprising way when touched or moved, for example, a Newton's cradle, a wind-up toy or electronic device. Ask everyone to watch how it responds and talk about the process. You can't make it happen just by watching. You have to do something. The device responds.

On Peter's adventure with God, he got into trouble for talking about Jesus and was put in prison. God's people, the church, could not do anything about it so they did the only thing they could do. They prayed. We don't know what they prayed, but we do know that God responded. Read Acts 12:1–19 to share the story.

Using the device again, make the point that when something troubles us and we cannot do much about it, the one thing we can do is pray. (Start your device.) God is unlike our machines and devices, however. We do not know *how* he will respond, but we do know that he *will* respond in a loving way when we pray.

Song suggestions

'And can it be?' *SOF* 21
'We are his people' *ts* 538
'Ask! Ask! Ask!' *JP* 11
'God has made me' *JP* 346
'Hear my mouth speak' *SOF* 1260
'You are the King of glory' *SOF* 1652

Prayer idea

Give out cuttings from local or national newspapers. Provide a mixture of positive and negative stories or pictures. Invite everyone to use the cuttings during the week as a prompt for prayer. Remind everyone that God responds when we pray. Though we cannot control how he responds, we can be sure he will do something good! You could break into small groups to pray, or a couple of people could lead in prayer.

Extra idea

It would be appropriate to contact a mission partner to ask them how you could pray for them in this service. Make sure there are visual images to introduce them and the topics. If possible, communicate directly with them during the service. People could send email messages at the end of the service, with photographic attachments, to demonstrate that as partners, they are still part of the church family. You can rejoice with them at how God answers prayer.

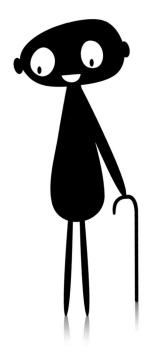

Elijah the prophet

The incomparable power of the Lord God is seen through the life of Elijah.

Learn and remember verse: 'God's Spirit fills us with power, love and self-control.' 2 Timothy 1:7

The song 'God's Spirit' from *Bitesize Bible Songs 2* CD (SU) puts these words to music and can be downloaded from www.scriptureunion.org.uk

The all-age service outline that is part of this series is 'Miraculous God' on page 118, focused on I Kings 17:17–24 and John 2:1–11.

July – Sept
10

Power to provide

Bible reading: I Kings 17
Session aim: To appreciate the life-giving power of God

Theme introduction

Prepare three glass jars. Put water in the first, bread in the second and leave the third empty. Explain that these jars contain the essentials for life.

Look at the water first. God gave the prophet Elijah water to drink even though there was a terrible drought. Discuss together God's gift of water and all the many ways in which we use it.

Show the second jar, saying that God provided bread for Elijah even though the lack of rain meant that no food crops were growing. Discuss God's gift of food and how essential it is for our lives.

Hold up the third empty jar and challenge people to think what it contains that is essential for life. Say that every breath we take fills our lungs with air. This too is God's gift for our lives. God showed his power in Elijah's experience by giving breath back to a boy who had died. Remind everyone that although we tend to take these essentials for granted, water, bread and air are the life-giving gifts of a powerful God.

Song suggestions

'You are worthy' *MP* 794
'Immortal, invisible' *ts* 220
'O Lord, you're great' *JP* 435
'Ah, Lord God' *SOF* 3
'Like the sunshine' *SOF* 1421
'Every breath I breathe' *SOF* 1224

Prayer idea

Pray for those who do not have an abundance of life essentials – for those who must drink dirty, contaminated water, for those who do not have enough to eat, for those who breathe unclean air or whose illness means they cannot breathe freely. Use this response: **Powerful God, we ask you to give life-giving water (food, breath) to all your children.**

Extra idea

Prepare a display which connects with this week's Bible passage. It could be placed on a blue drape. Suitable items would be bread, a photograph of a raven, water, a bowl of flour and some olive oil. These items could be brought forward as they are mentioned during the Bible reading. Invite the congregation to look at the display after the service and think of the ways in which God's power provides the essentials of their lives.

(This activity will be replicated in the next three sessions.)

Power to amaze

Bible reading: 1 Kings 18
Session aim: To recognise God as the one all-powerful Lord

Theme introduction

Think about who has the most power in your own community – in schools, in local government, in the streets and so on. It may be an individual, a certain section of society, a pressure group or organisation. Establish that powerful people have influence on the whole community, for good or ill.

Demonstrate the power struggle in Elijah's time. Imagine that you are living in Samaria (the northern kingdom of Israel). Two volunteers can represent King Ahab and Queen Jezebel. Jezebel worshipped a god called Baal who doesn't really exist. She was so powerful that she persuaded Ahab to abandon his worship of the real God. Baal's 'prophets' encouraged people in the whole country to worship Baal. (Recruit a number of volunteers to stand with Ahab and Jezebel.) Who would be brave enough not only to worship God, but to stand up against the king and queen?

Elijah was that brave person. Stand one person opposite the group already formed, looking alone and powerless. Who looks more powerful? Who is really more powerful? Elijah was about to show everyone that God was much more powerful than Baal, Baal's prophets and those who worshipped Baal!

Song suggestions

'O worship the King' *MP* 528
'Holy, holy, holy, Lord God Almighty!' *SOF* 183
'Among the gods' *ts* 19
'God of glory, we exalt your name' *ts* 130
'Our God is so great' ('My God is so big') *ts* 420
'Jesus, be the centre' *SOF* 1377

Prayer idea

God of fire, God of power, you are the one true God.
God of wind, God of power, you are the only Lord of our lives.
God of drenching rain, God of power, we will follow you.
God of power, may we know your power even when we feel powerless.

Extra idea

Prepare a display which connects with this week's Bible story. It could be placed on a red drape. Suitable items would be photographs of clouds, four jars of water, firewood, twelve large stones and some way of representing fire (perhaps candles, if this can be done safely, or a lamp). These items could be brought forward as they are mentioned during the Bible reading. Invite the congregation to look at the display after the service and think about the way in which God showed himself to be the one all-powerful God.

The power to protect

Bible reading: 1 Kings 19:1−21

Session aim: To discover that God's power is at work in us even when we want to give up

Theme introduction

Invite two volunteers to play a simple game visible to everyone. A giant version of a game such as *Jenga* or *Connect 4* would be ideal. Otherwise use the following game which needs no special equipment, just 20 large items (books, pieces of fruit, plastic cups) which are placed between the players. The players take turns to choose whether to remove one, two or three items. The object is to force the other player to take the last item away.

There will come a moment when one player is obviously on the verge of losing. Stop the game and ask this player if they would like to give up. Depending on the answer, congratulate him or her on having the courage to continue or say that you understand why they don't want to.

Most people want to give up sometimes. Give a few examples: when work seems hard, when we've had no success for a long time, when other people tell us we will never be any good. What keeps us going when we want to give up − courage, determination, faith? You could refer back to how Peter kept going when in prison; see page 57 (JS7).

Remind everyone that God is still the same powerful God even when *we* want to give up. This is what Elijah discovered when he thought he was the only one who was still loyal to God. God helped him see that he was not alone, not powerless and not without hope.

Song suggestions

'Praise my soul, the King of heaven' *SOF* 466
'He is the Lord (Show your power)' *ts* 159
'What a mighty God we serve' *JP* 491
'God of glory' *SOF* 137
'Draw me closer' *SOF* 1216
'How great are you, Lord' *SOF* 1291

Prayer idea

Pray for Christians whose circumstances make it difficult to believe and who may feel like giving up. For instance, those whose families or friends make fun of their beliefs; those who face persecution; those who cannot find a job or have a long-term illness.

Extra idea

Prepare a display which connects with this week's Bible story. It could be placed on a brown or yellow drape. Suitable items would be a photograph of a mountain, a jar of water, some bread and a piece of fabric to represent a cloak. These items could be brought forward as they are mentioned during the Bible reading. Invite the congregation to look at the display after the service and think about the one all-powerful God.

The power to judge

Bible reading: 1 Kings 21:1–19; 22:29–40
Session aim: To see that even powerful people aren't as powerful as God

Theme introduction

In advance, ask two people (adults or older children) to prepare a minute's talk about who they think is the most powerful person in the world and why. (Make sure they choose different people!) Introduce these talks by saying that the congregation is going to decide which of the two they think is the most powerful person in the world The choice will be theirs!

Invite the speakers to give their talks, encouraging a round of applause for each one. Then take a vote and declare the winner 'The world's most powerful person!' This was hardly a fair vote as there were only two candidates, but it does show some of the qualities that make people powerful.

Together compile a list of the qualities of powerful people. What good things can they do? What bad things? King Ahab and his wife, Jezebel, were very powerful in Samaria. They thought they had the power to do what they liked. Elijah was brave enough to stand up to them and tell them that, compared to God, their power was very limited. They learnt that power is not for getting your own way. God's power is awesome, but it is always fair and used for good.

Song suggestions

'Rejoice, the Lord is King!' *SOF* 482
'God is our strength and refuge' *MP* 188
'Ascribe greatness' *ts* 25
'Show your power, O Lord' *ts* 454
'Who is like you?' *SOF* 1621
'Praise him, you heavens' *SOF* 1501

Prayer idea

Use Psalm 111 which sums up many of the themes of the series on Elijah. To ensure participation as the psalm is read, pick out key words, for example, 'wonderful', 'majesty', 'power' and 'mighty', according to the version you are using, and ask everyone to clap or cheer when they hear those words.

Extra idea

Prepare a display which connects with the first section of this week's Bible story (1 Kings 21:1–19). It could be placed on a green drape. Suitable items would be vine leaves (real or download an image), a large bunch of grapes, two crowns to represent Ahab and Jezebel and some (fake) money. These items could be brought forward as they are mentioned during the Bible reading. Invite the congregation to look at the display after the service and think about powerful people and their powerlessness compared to God.

(As this is the last session in the Elijah series you could show all the items you have displayed and use this to refresh memories of what you have discovered about God's power.)

PART TWO

All-age service outlines

These 15 service outlines have followed the tested format of Scripture Union's *Light for the Lectionary* books and earlier material from *Light Years* and *Salt for all ages*. There are a number of options which may not all work for your situation or tradition and there may be too much for one service. All-age services are usually fairly creative so one suggestion in this book may stimulate several of your own ideas.

Each service outline contains the following:

Aims: keep these in mind throughout the service to ensure that you are clear in what you are exploring. Of course, you may wish to rephrase them, but don't lose sight of your own aims. Clear aims help to evaluate the service.

Getting started: some background information sets the outline and its content in a wider context. This also alerts a service leader to any issues that might arise.

You will need: preparing for all-age services is time-consuming but this checklist should be useful. Necessary downloads are listed and alternatives are usually suggested for those who do not use the Internet. All downloads are available on the Scripture Union website: www.scriptureunion.org.uk/light and listed in service order.

Beginning the service: it is important to start well. These suggestions are varied in style and if one option would not work for you, the suggestion in another service could spark an alternative idea. Aim right from the start to create some sense of community.

Bible reading: almost all outlines include an Old Testament and a New Testament reading, even though only one of these may be the focus of the service. Public reading of the Bible is vitally important and it needs to be done in a way that captures the attention of all present. Creative suggestions are given throughout the 15 outlines. Occasional suggestions have been given for **Bible retelling**.

Bible talk: plenty of interactivity has been built into the Bible talk, recognising that people learn in different ways. The basic framework is given but the speaker will need to adapt to their own style and circumstances.

Prayer activity: communicating with God can be done in many different ways. The suggestions in the outlines involve activity for individuals and more corporately. But do not forget that sometimes we need to meet with God in stillness.

Prayers of confession: church traditions vary in how much emphasis they place specifically on acknowledging our sin and seeking God's forgiveness. This is one option that may fit in with your regular style or it may be something quite different that you could explore further.

Prayers of intercession: outsiders expect Christians to pray for them and the world in need. It is valuable to include people of all ages in leading these prayers, some of which are very active and some less so.

Ending the service: a good ending is important since it sends people out on their way into the world having a clear sense of what God has been saying to them and his people.

Helpful extras: the songbooks that are used suggested in **Music and song ideas** are listed on page 11 but this list is not comprehensive.

A **Statement of faith** may not be part of your tradition but it is a useful means of drawing people together in a resolve to know and serve God. **Games** are suggested, some of which are available as downloads. These are especially important for providing for young children and anyone whose preferred learning style is of a more active nature.

Notes and comments: extra ideas and explanation may help you in your preparation. Extra ideas of course are also available in Part One, in the starter suggestions, linked to the *Light* theme you are exploring.

Downloads: these are to be found on the Scripture Union website www.scriptureunion. org.uk/light. A download is referenced according to the volume (AASA4.) the month if you were using it in the Light cycle (Oct), and then consecutive numbers (_2) - for example AASA4.Oct_2. The downloads include word documents providing necessary templates or scripts as well as PowerPoint presentations or video clips.

Golden rules for all-age worship

The foundational key for leading effective all-age worship is thinking about it as a family time (the church family), not as a time for the children with the adults present, or as an adult worship time with the children present. It's an all-age time – a totally unique 'brand' of worship.

This three-point checklist will help you in your planning worship when all ages are present.

1. Is it appropriate?
Is what I am planning – simple and uncomplicated? It should be!
Is what I am planning – childish or embarrassing or patronising? It should NOT be.

Example: language is one thing to be really aware of. It needs to be simple and clear, although the concept may be understood on several levels.
NOT: Let's come before the Lord in penitence for our transgressions.
NOT: Now we're going to say sorry for the naughty things we've done.
BUT: We're going to spend some time saying sorry to God for the things we've done wrong.
(Simple, uncomplicated language that connects with everyone.)

2. Is it moving at the right pace?
Variety is crucial, (fast-moving and busy, reflective and still) and it is not necessarily older people who like stillness and vice versa!
As a general rule, aim for one activity to last no longer than seven minutes.

3. How much interaction is there?
Option 1: interaction between the leader and congregation
Option 2: interaction amongst the congregation
Option 3: interaction between the congregation and God

Interaction should never be forced upon anyone and should never be artificial or for the sake of 'doing something'. Never separate an activity into say 'a song for the children' for that will alienate adults. Instead, for example, say, 'We'll sing another song now.'

Examples: movement; singing and making music (and repetition helps the youngest to the oldest join in); stories; puppets; sign language; using all the senses; mime; construction/craft; engaging with symbols and artefacts; humour and emotion.

As a service leader
• Remember that you are leading people together into God's presence
• Be enthusiastic and enjoy yourself
• Prepare well and work with others
• Never be apologetic for what you are leading

This has been adapted from *Golden rules for all-age worship* by Jo Squires
© 2008 BIG Ministries www.bigministries.co.uk and used with permission.

Harvest gatherers

October

Light series: The challenge of following Jesus
Light readings: Luke 4:16−30; 5:17−26; 7:36−50; 10:38−42;
Isaiah 61:1,2

Aims: to hear how Jesus sent his disciples into the harvest
to be challenged to gather others to Jesus

Readings: Luke 10:1−12, Psalm 67

Getting started

The *Light* series in October, based on Luke's Gospel, explores Jesus' declaration of his kingdom manifesto (taken from Isaiah 61), and how his healing and forgiveness turned this manifesto into action. The Old Testament offers hints and clues about the Messiah − the chosen or promised one of Israel. Many in Israel at the time of Jesus expected that the Messiah would be a great warrior, a mighty king who would drive the Romans out of Israel. However, by focusing on the vision Isaiah had of a suffering servant, Jesus not only undermined common perceptions, but tipped their expectations upside down.

We must also live as those in God's kingdom! Jesus took children, blessed them and accepted what they offered. God has always given children challenging (but achievable) tasks to complete. In this service, we must treat children of all ages seriously as believers, encouraging and developing them as Jesus did. It may be that you will use this service as the basis for an 'alternative harvest festival' − with a spiritual rather than physical harvest being celebrated. If so, remember that the most fruitful harvest field in the world is amongst under 18s, so you are equipping the workers to go into that potentially fruitful harvest field.

You will need

- a volunteer with a rucksack, passport, atlas, compass, garden spade or fork, pruning shears, trug/basket, clothes and a wash bag − for **Beginning the service** and **Ending the service**
- Psalm 67 on display or printed for an antiphonal **Bible reading** (AASA4.Oct_1)
- the script (AASA4.Oct_2), props and four actors for the **Bible retelling** drama of Luke 10:1−12
- flip chart and pen for the **Bible talk**
- **Statement of faith,** (AASA4.Oct_3), on screen or printed
- coffee cup or bag of sweets and a picture of an ear for **Ending the service**

All downloads are freely available from www.scriptureunion.org.uk/lightdownloads.

Beginning the service

With: music if appropriate; volunteer explorer with rucksack containing passport, atlas, compass, garden tools, basket, wash bag, spare clothes

Welcome everyone and, if you usually start with a song, sing something like 'Come let us sing of a wonderful love' or 'Go forth and tell'. After this, someone dressed in 'explorer' clothes, carrying a rucksack, wanders to the front calling, 'I'm ready! I'm ready!' Find out where they are going, what they think they are doing and why they are in church. From the rucksack pull out the following: a passport, atlas and compass (because they might be going anywhere); spade or fork; pruning shears and basket (because they are going to gather a harvest) and regular travel items like clothes and a wash bag. Make this as amusing as possible.

Thank the 'explorer' and say that it isn't that kind of harvest that you're going to talk about today. Keep the rucksack at the front for **Ending the service**.

Bible reading

Psalm 67 lends itself to an antiphonal reading. A PowerPoint version (AASA4.Oct_1) is available. Split the congregation into two groups.

A: May God be gracious to us and bless us
B: *and make his face shine on us —*
A: so that your ways may be known on earth
B: *your salvation among all nations.*
A: May the peoples praise you, God;
B: *may all the peoples praise you.*
A: May the nations be glad and sing for joy, for you rule the peoples with equity
B: *and guide the nations of the earth.*
A: May the peoples praise you, God;
B: *may all the peoples praise you.*
A: The land yields its harvest;
B: *God, our God, blesses us.*
All: May God bless us still, so that all the ends of the earth will fear him.

Bible retelling

A script for a drama based on Luke 10:1–12 (AASA4.Oct_2) is available. It is for four characters – Jesus and three of the 72 disciples. You will need a sign or Powerpoint slide with the words: 'Harvest Preparation Strategy Group', a table with notebooks or files and four chairs.

Bible talk

With: flip chart and pen; someone to give their personal testimony

Put people into groups of four or five to come up with ideas of what one thing they might ask Jesus for if he walked into church today. After a couple of minutes, encourage feedback from people of different ages, making a list on the flip chart. Affirm all answers, even if some are surprising! Suggestions might include: healing, forgiveness, a big brother, a chance to play for United, the dead to come back to life, acceptance, love, understanding, salvation, justice, sight, guidance. Then ask which of these are dependent on having money or resources.

Explain that Jesus and his 72 disciples did not need money or things to show that the kingdom of God was at hand. What they needed was an openness for the Spirit of God to work through them so that they could bring God's blessing to others. They needed to depend on God to lead them to the right places. They had to step out and get on with the business of telling others about him. They took nothing with them and had to trust that people would feed and shelter them.

This call to tell others about Jesus and to depend on God is true for us. The world is still hungry for God's good news, but it is easy to think that we will be rejected or people will laugh at us. But however tough it may be, God is with us and sharing Jesus is a real privilege and adventure. Ask what might be stopping people from sharing what they know of God – fear, lack of confidence, independence…?

In advance, prepare someone to give their testimony of a simple sharing of the good news in word or action. This might be coffee with a friend, taking food to a bereaved person, digging a neighbour's garden or sharing the gospel in conversation with a friend or colleague. Ask them to explain how they overcame any reluctance to speak or act, and also what kind of reaction they got from the person they shared with.

We don't have to be rich, or clever, or extraordinary to share what we know of God or to act in his name. We need to be gentle, kind, loving, forgiving and confident that God can do it through us. Ask everyone to think and decide who they can help.

Move straight into the **Prayers of intercession**.

Prayers of intercession

Ask everyone to stand. Then pray as follows:

Three in one God, we ask you to work through us as we remember three sets of people.

Show us those we can speak to in your name.
(*Everyone holds up their index finger to represent someone to whom they can say something kind today, which includes speaking to them about Jesus. Pause to think who this might be.*)

Show us people we can serve in your name this week.
(*Everyone holds up both thumbs to represent two people they could help in a practical way this week. Pause to think who this might be.*)

Show us people who do not live near us, who need to hear from us in your name this week.
(*Everyone holds up a little finger to represent people who live far away. Pause to think who this might be.*)

Thank you that your love and mercy are without end.
Thank you that your good news is for all people.
Thank you that you invite us to accept the challenge to share your love and power.
Give us courage to speak,
Give us courage to act,
to spread your news and your kingdom with others.
Amen

Prayer activity

The 72 disciples went around talking about what Jesus had said and done. It may not have been done eloquently, but telling others was what it was all about. What would people in church today want to tell others about Jesus?

(The answer to this question might be quite a challenge for people who are not used to being reflective. It would help if you could give some examples of what you mean – such as an answer to prayer, a resolution to what seemed an impossible dilemma, the words that someone said to you which reflected God's activity or something you were able to say which in retrospect was just the right thing.)

In small groups of two or three, ask everyone to think of the following and then share it with their partner(s).

What one thing has God done for you this last week?
What is the best thing for you about being a friend of Jesus?
If appropriate, the small groups link arms to pray for one another, that they will all be able to share what they know about Jesus with others this coming week.

Ending the service

With: the rucksack of equipment from **Beginning the service**, a coffee cup or bag of sweets, a picture of an ear

Take the atlas out of the rucksack and remind people they won't need a map to find their harvest field – it is right where they are; at school, home and work. Take out the spade or fork and remind them they might need this if the best way for them to love a neighbour is by doing their garden! Then hold up the coffee cup or bag of sweets and suggest that sharing these with a friend or neighbour might be the first step to a meaningful friendship where they can see God at work, enabling the person to be willing to hear about Jesus.

Hold up the picture of the ear and suggest that in order to earn the right to speak, we ourselves must first listen. Jesus always asked people what they wanted and met that need before telling them about the kingdom. Challenge everyone to do the same this week.

Helpful extras

Music and song ideas

'Go forth and tell' *SOF* 738
'Come let us sing of a wonderful love' *SOF* 72
'How lovely on the mountains' *SOF* 192
'Tell out my soul' *SOF* 520
'Meekness and Majesty' *SOF* 120
'Forth in thy name' *SOF* 1237
'One shall tell another' *SOF* 439
'Jesus Christ is waiting' *SOF* 1381
'I the Lord of sea and sky' *SOF* 830
'Wow' *RU*

Statement of faith

This statement (AASA4.Oct_3) is also available online.

Lord your news is good news!
It is good news for us!
It is good news for our family!
It is good news for our friends!
It is good news for our neighbours!
It is good news for strangers!
It is good news for our enemies!
Give us boldness to share it!
Alleluia!

Notes and comments

If you have a parade service, ask members of the uniformed groups to talk about how they try to put their promise into practice in serving others.

Make sure that you pray for any in the church family who are committed to sharing the good news of Jesus in a particular way, in the locality or further away. If you have any charity workers, service professionals or councillors within the congregation, you could interview them about ways the church can help serve the community or service users of the charity. This might lead to a working party examining the feasibility of projects such as a Court Contact Centre, a listening ear drop-in or something similar.
If Psalm 67 seems short, you could substitute Psalm 103 as an antiphonal reading.

Decision-making

November

Light series: Hearing from God
Light readings: I Samuel 1:1–2:21; 2:22–3:21; 7:3 – 8:9; 12;15

Aims: to hear how God communicated with Samuel when he chose Saul to be king
to think how God helps us to make decisions

Readings: I Samuel 9,10; Acts 16:6–10

Getting started

During November the *Light* series focuses on the story of Samuel: how Hannah prayed for a baby and then dedicated her new son to God's service; how young Samuel learned to respond to God's voice; how Samuel, the holy man, encouraged the people of Israel to listen to God through prayer and by fasting; and how Samuel worked alongside Saul.

How do we make decisions? The world encourages people to make decisions on the basis of luck, advice from experts or their own ability to think things through. Many people needing to make a decision can be easily overwhelmed by too much choice.

This service explores godly yet practical ways of making decisions – by listening to God's voice, by following his guidance and seeing where he is already directing opportunities in life. The story of how Saul and his servant decided to consult Samuel, a man of God, gives some indications of the different ways Christians can make decisions.

Acts 16:6–10 provides a further example of Christian decision-making as Paul's vision enabled him to make a decision about where he was going to preach next.

You will need

- 'Twister' game for **Beginning the service**
- seven volunteers to read I Samuel 9,10 in the **Bible reading**
- the script (AASA4.Nov_1) for the **Bible retelling**
- a smart briefcase containing a coin, a dice, a TV programme guide and a newspaper horoscope for the **Bible talk**
- materials for the **Prayer activity**

All downloads are freely available from www.scriptureunion.org.uk/lightdownloads.

Beginning the service

With: a game of Twister (A giant version would be fun for a mix of children and adults if there is enough space for the mat, though the standard version will work just as well.)

Set the game going so that all the players have had at least two turns. As they continue to play, ask those watching how the players know what move to make next. Ask if it is an easy game to play. The answer is likely to be 'Yes' in the early stages and 'No' once the mat is full of bodies stretching across each other. Ask if the game could be played in any other way.

Halt the game, offering a further chance to play after the service. Ask the players if they had to make any decisions during the game. They may say 'No' because they were instructed where to place their foot or hand. If that is the case, point out that they had to decide how to get their foot or hand to a vacant spot to put it down.

Every day, people have to make hundreds, if not thousands, of decisions. What are good ways to make those decisions? Do we listen to other people and get into a knot, like those playing Twister? What does it mean to take guidance from God?

Learn or practise the Learn and remember verse: 'The Lord is like a strong tower, where the righteous can go and be safe.' (Proverbs 18:10). For a song version see **Music and song ideas**.

Bible reading

Use a modern version of the Bible to read these verses: 1 Samuel 9:1–6, 14–21, 24b–27; 10:1, 9–16. Different readers could take the parts of Kish, Saul, the servant, the Lord, Samuel, and Saul's uncle, plus a narrator.

Before reading Acts 16: 6–10, explain that Paul spent years travelling across the countries of the Middle East to tell people the good news of Jesus. He listened to the instructions of the Holy Spirit, rather than just going to the places that he, Paul, wanted to visit. Here is how he got on during one of his journeys.

Bible retelling

Tell the story of Saul meeting Samuel, using the script (AASA4.Nov_1). Encourage everyone to join in the descriptions of Saul and Samuel each time their names are mentioned.

Bible talk

With: a smart briefcase containing a coin, a dice, a TV programme guide and a newspaper horoscope

Show the briefcase and explain that it contains all the current wisdom from the latest research on decision-making. All of these decision-making tools are used regularly.

Take out the coin and ask how a coin can help make a decision. Tossing a coin or 'heads or tails' is a familiar way to decide between two options. Flip the coin into the air and ask when people have seen it done – the answer may be at the beginning of a football or cricket match.

Next show the dice. Ask which games children have played that use a dice.
The answer will relate to games of chance, indicating how many moves to take, for example.

Some people make decisions by reading their horoscope (*bring out the example*), but the Bible tells us not to do that. So that has to be rejected. (*Throw it away.*)

Point out that people often have difficulty in deciding which television programme to watch – but help is at hand. Show the TV programme guide and explain that there is usually a brief description of the programmes to help everyone to decide. A bit more information can help make a decision.

Rolling a dice is helpful when playing a board game but it does not help in deciding which job to apply for, where to live or how much money to give to charity. Tossing a coin may be simple but it just demonstrates chance. The TV programme guide gives some information, but still requires us to make the decision. So what is God's way to make a decision?

Invite a member of a Christian family to give their testimony briefly about how they recently made up their mind in a significant decision. When asking them to contribute beforehand, ensure that they will emphasise the importance of prayer, and possibly confirmation from other people, among other factors.

The **Bible reading** was about a string of decisions – and proofs that God was directing what was happening. (If appropriate, ask people to look up the verses in their Bibles.)
• The servant advised Saul to consult Samuel,

the man of God, and Saul agreed (9:6).

- Samuel had listened to God when God said that a stranger (Saul) would appear (9:15).
- Samuel decided to obey God's instruction to anoint Saul as king (9:16; 10:1).
- Samuel gave Saul three signs, or clear indications, so that Saul would understand that God was with him – and they happened:

1 Saul met people who told him that the donkeys had been found (10:2)
2 Saul was given two loaves of bread (10:4)
3 Saul met the dancing prophets (10:5)

Here are four top tips for Christian decision-making, similar to the decisions Samuel and Saul made:

1 Talking with God and listening carefully to his voice.
2 Seeking advice from the right people.
3 Being prepared to follow God's instructions.
4 Looking out for signs of answered prayer.

If you have read Acts 16:6–10, remind everyone that Paul changed his travel and preaching plans because of a clear vision, or dream. He had learned to listen to God, to recognise his voice, and to be prepared to follow the instructions.

Prayer activity

Set up four prayer areas, based on the four top tips above: Listen to God, Listen to others, Follow God's instructions, Look for answered prayer. Each area will need an instruction card (AASA4.Nov_2). Invite everyone to visit as many of the prayer areas as they choose. Indicate how much time will be available for this. Quiet background music will dull the noise of people moving around.

Listen to God
Provide small trays of sand for people to finger gently as they are quiet in God's presence. Display a card with the following words on it:

Samuel looked at Saul, and the Lord told Samuel, 'This is the man I told you about. He's the one who will rule Israel.' Ask God what he wants to say to you today.

Listen to others
Provide paper and pens. On card, display the following words:

The servant advised Saul. Write the names or draw the people whom you trust the most, people who give you wise advice. Pray for these wise people.

Follow God's instructions
Provide a supply of colourful chenille sticks (pipe cleaners) and display the following words on a card:

'Wait!' the servant answered. 'There's a man of God who lives in a town near here…Maybe he can tell us where to look.' Reflect on one thing God is calling you to do and shape a chenille stick to represent that.

Suggest that people walk round the worship space holding the stick and praying about God's call. When they return to the area, they could pick up a second, different-coloured stick if they are willing to follow God's call and entwine the two sticks together as a sign of this.

Look for answered prayer
Provide a range of photographs of stories in the news, cut from newspapers or downloaded from the Internet. Suggest everyone picks up one photograph. They could discuss what they see with someone else and pray together. On card, display the following words:

Kish told Saul, 'Take one of the servants and go to look for the donkeys.' Where is God in this story? Can you see where God is in the story of the photograph you are holding? How has God answered prayer?

Once everyone is back in their places, gather up everyone's prayers by saying the Learn and remember verse together (Proverbs 18:10).

Prayers of intercession

Practise the Learn and remember verse again: 'The Lord is like a strong tower, where the righteous can go and be safe.' (Proverbs 18:10). This verse will be used as a response during the prayers. It reminds everyone that people who look to the Lord can be safe to be helped to make wise decisions.

Pray for everyone who has to exercise responsibility as a leader – the Prime Minister and members of Parliament; everyone who serves on the local council or authority (use the correct local term); head teachers; people who run businesses and organisations.
The Lord is like a strong tower, where the righteous can go and be safe.

Pray for church leaders, including everyone who leads groups for children and young people.

The Lord is like a strong tower, where the righteous can go and be safe.

Pray for parents and everyone who looks after children or cares for people in need.
The Lord is like a strong tower, where the righteous can go and be safe.

Pray for people who have to make difficult decisions at the moment about work or money or family life.
The Lord is like a strong tower, where the righteous can go and be safe.

Pray for ourselves, that we may turn to the Lord for guidance in all important decisions we have to make this week.
The Lord is like a strong tower, where the righteous can go and be safe.

Ending the service

Remind everyone that we all have to make decisions every day – what clothes to wear, whether to watch television or play with a computer game, how to spend our money. Some decisions are small and others are so big that we are scared of making the wrong decision. The story of Saul and Samuel demonstrates that we can look to God for guidance if we listen for his voice (and often he guides us through the advice of others), look for the signs that show that he is already sorting things out and follow his instructions. Challenge everyone to make their decisions on this basis in the next few days.

Helpful extras

Music and song ideas

'Faithful One' *SOF* 89
'Great is thy faithfulness' *SOF* 147
'Guide me, O thou great Jehovah' *SOF* 148
'Oh, lead me' *SOF* 956
'Though I feel afraid' *SOF* 1063
'Strong tower' *BSBS* – the Learn and remember verse for Proverbs 18:10

Game

Use the Twister game, but after everyone who is playing has had at least one turn, substitute another dice. Make a small sign for each face of the dice, with one each of these instructions:
- Stop and pray
- Be still and know that I am God
- Look around for signs of God at work
- Listen to God's Holy Spirit
- Do what God is calling you to do
- Consult a Christian friend

After a few turns, discuss why the game is not progressing. Ask what decisions these instructions would help with.

Notes and comments

It is possible to start playing Twister as soon as people start arriving. This could let more children and young people have a turn, as well as giving them something to do whilst waiting for the formal start.

Children and adults who are unused to 'active' prayers may need some help to take part in the **Prayer activity**. Either encourage parents to accompany their children to each prayer area, or arrange for at least one person to 'host' the area to explain how to take part. Also point out that some people may prefer to remain in their places to pray quietly. This is just as valid a choice as visiting the prayer areas.

For the **Prayer activity**, buy 'play' sand from a toyshop. It can be stored in a large container after use and brought out on a future occasion (for example Harvest, see Session 15). Clean food trays, such as those which contain vegetables or fruit, make good free containers for the sand. These can be stored for future use. The sand does not have to be deep, but just sufficient to cover the base of the container so that patterns can be drawn in it. Chenille sticks (or pipe cleaners) can be obtained from most toyshops or Internet craft suppliers.

Decision-making is a challenge and may particularly be so at this time of year when choices are made about secondary schools. The prayer team could be available to pray for others after the service. This is a way of demonstrating to visitors, as well as church members, that guidance in God's name is available. No one has to make a decision on their own.

Jesus for the whole world

December

Light series: God is love
Light readings: Isaiah 7:14; 9:2−7; 60:1−3; John 1:1−18; Matthew 1:18−25; 2:1−12; Luke 2:1−20; Micah 5:2−5

Aims: to explore the far-reaching impact of Christmas – Jesus came for all peoples, in every place, and for all time
to emphasise that we are looking forward to Jesus

Readings: Isaiah 60:1−3; John 1:1−18

Getting started

The theme of this month's *Light* series is 'God is love', taking time to wonder that God loves us so much that he became a human. His coming had a profound effect on all the characters involved in the event itself but, as we know, it also has eternal significance, for all people, throughout time.

This session builds on this, looking at how God showed his love for the whole world as 'the Word became a human being and lived here with us' (John 1:14, CEV). At the beginning of the season of Advent the service brings together a number of truths about Jesus' coming (incarnation), looking forward to the period of Christmas. But this service also has a dimension beyond 25th December this year for we know Jesus is coming a second time. Isaiah's words in Isaiah 60:1−3 hint at that.

This is an opportunity to broaden many people's understanding of Advent, which can often be little more than opening a calendar door for the first 24 days of December to find a hidden chocolate! Isaiah 60:1−3 and John 1:1−18 form the backbone to the session. The activities encourage groups of all ages to work together, so ensure children and older people contribute as much as possible.

You will need

• an Advent wreath and lighter
• a video of the rising sun – 'ambient DVDs' will provide this (eg. www.naturedvd.co.uk) or a photograph of a sunrise plus a reflective/classical CD track for **Beginning the service**
• A selection of instruments or a digital music writing programme and laptop computer; a musical accompaniment to the **Bible reading** prepared in advance
• for the **Bible talk,** silk scarves, flags, ribbons, fabric or any other coloured material; candles and lighters; optional black card; A4 sheets or flipchart paper with pens; A4 paper folded into fans, scissors and staplers; PowerPoint images or photos of the human emotions of different people across the world (AASA4.Dec_1)
• country or continent-shaped paper (template – AASA4.Dec_2); pens for **Prayer activity**
• optional track from Taizé CD or MP3 for **Prayers of intercession**

All downloads are freely available from www.scriptureunion.org.uk/lightdownloads.

Beginning the service

Encourage the congregation to come to worship in a spirit of quietness. Begin by playing a video of the sun rising, starting with darkness and rising to light, or showing a photograph of a sunrise on the screen. Play a reflective CD track to accompany this as the scene is set for the service. If no technical equipment is available, play the music while encouraging participants to close their eyes and imagine the sun rising, bringing in the dawn of a new day. Light the Advent wreath if this is your custom during Advent. Follow this by reading out loud Isaiah 60:3 then invite everyone to worship in the words of the hymn 'Tell out my soul'.

Bible reading

Before reading Isaiah 60:1–3, explain that the writer is speaking of the future of Jerusalem which has come to stand for the place and time when God will make himself known across the world.

For dramatic effect, accompany the reading with 'live' instruments. Encourage musicians to be creative. Band instruments or those borrowed from a local Primary school would be effective. The accompaniment should be rehearsed. Alternatively, with more advance notice, invite some young people to prepare a digital accompaniment to the reading using 'EJay', 'Garageband' or another digital music programme. This can be played from a computer through speakers as the passage is read. If the 'sunrise' video or photograph idea has been used, continue to display it as a visual reminder that a 'new day is dawning' as Jesus comes to earth.

> Jerusalem, stand up! Shine! Your new day is dawning. The glory of the LORD shines brightly on you. (*Use a drum kit or a cymbal shimmer using soft beaters.*)
>
> The earth and its people are covered with darkness, (*Slow use of a rainmaker or bass drum; if chime bars are available, play combinations of notes which create a dark sound.*) but the glory of the LORD is shining upon you. (*Use triangles and tambourines.*)
>
> Nations and kings will come to the light of your dawning day. (*Fanfare on a keyboard and/or trumpet.*)
>
> Isaiah 60:1–3 (CEV)

Bible talk

This talk will take everyone on a journey following the work of God in the world from the beginning of time through to the life of Jesus. The journey's guide is John 1:1–18 and will be a series of experiences and activities to illuminate God's Word.

The beginning
With: all necessary props

Begin with a dramatic reading of John 1:1–4. Using silk scarves, flags, ribbons, fabric or any other coloured material, invite members of the congregation to wave, move or dance, using the materials of relevant colours as follows:
Verses 1,2: *White or any other 'neutral' colour.*
Verse 3: *Introduce colours one at a time, to represent the different aspects of creation: blue; turquoise or blue/green; silver or white; green; brown; rainbow or multi-coloured fabric.*
Verse 4: *Yellow/gold.*

Share briefly that God had a plan for his world and that what he created was beautiful, stunning and full of variety and colour. God (Father, Son and Spirit) were there at the beginning, involved in creation and have always been part of the world throughout history. (*Light three candles, to represent the Trinity. This is not to be confused with the lighting of the candles in an Advent wreath.*)

The darkness
Using a black PowerPoint slide or a large piece of black card, explain that because human beings chose to disobey God, the world became 'dark'. Wrong things changed the world from being perfect to being a place which was not as God intended. People over many centuries forgot about God, but God never left or gave up on his world. As the candles continue to burn, God is still in the world.
Read John 1:5 and illustrate this by taking a flame from the three main candles lit in the first part of the **Bible talk** to light small candles spread around the church to represent the ever-present 'light' of God. (*Be careful to place candles carefully and in a way that children will not be burnt by wax*).

Looking forward to the coming of the Word
God never left his world and he always longed that people would 'know him' personally. For this to happen, he needed to become a person and live an ordinary life as an ordinary human being. This was the incarnation and was spoken about

over many years throughout the Old Testament. Remind everyone that Advent is a time of 'looking forward' to Christmas and also to the time when Jesus will come again. Refer back to the reading from Isaiah 60. Invite people of all ages to talk about the aspects of Christmas they are looking forward to. Highlight the fact that the passage in John shows us others in the past who looked forward to the coming of Christ to the world.

Read John 1:6-9 then split the congregation into groups – either in half or smaller groups depending on the size of the congregation and the mix of ages. Here are two activities which illustrate 'looking forward' to the coming of Christ.

Either: look up and read the following Bible verses, writing the name of the 'prophet' and a summary of each verse in different speech bubbles on sheets of paper: Exodus 3:14; Isaiah 7:14; Isaiah 9:2–7; Micah 5:2–5; Jeremiah 23:5; Psalm 22:30. Identify how close these verses are to what we know of Jesus in the New Testament.

Or: make a series of 'paper chain people' by folding A4 sheets into a fan, cutting out the shape of a person and stapling the 'people' together to make one long chain. You could refer to the genealogy passage in Matthew 1:1–12, or just ask people to think of those who lived in Old Testament times, most of whom would have been anticipating the coming of the Messiah in some shape or form. Write their names on an individual 'person' in the paper chain. (If you have access to the Scripture Union *Bible Timeline*, show that and talk about all the characters in the Old Testament.)

Jesus came
Read John 1:10–18 and emphasise verse 14: 'The Word became a human being and lived here with us. We saw his true glory, the glory of the only Son of the Father. From him all the kindness and all the truth of God have come down to us' (CEV). Explain that in his time on earth, Jesus was fully God but also fully human. He experienced human situations and emotions.

At this point, show images of people across the world who are experiencing a variety of emotions, ones that Jesus would have experienced. This could be done by showing photos or with the PowerPoint (AASA4.Dec_1). The emotions could include hunger (40 days in the wilderness), sadness (at the death of Lazarus), joy (as he spends time with his friends), betrayal (at the betrayal of Judas), tiredness (when he slept in a boat), fear (in the Garden of Gethsemane), physical pain (as he was crucified) and celebration (at a wedding). Jesus was 'one of us', just like us.

God so loved the world…
Conclude the **Bible talk** by explaining that, although Jesus did and said amazing things and made a difference to the lives of many people he met, the main reason for his coming was his death and resurrection. By dying and rising again, Jesus brought all peoples back to God so that they might experience his light in their life. He is the light for the church today across the world and the focus of the Christmas season.

Read John 3:16 and either sing it or learn it. Alternatively, learn the song 'The Word' as a Learn and remember verse for John 1:14 (see **Music and Song ideas**).

Prayer activity
With: small pieces of paper which are the distinctive shapes of countries or continents in the world – see AASA4.Dec_2 for a template, for example, Italy, Africa, Australia, Great Britain, India; pens; Blu-tack; a map of the world

Give each person a piece of paper and a pen and ask them to write or draw a word of thanks that Jesus came for the world. It could be something personal, something for the church or a general prayer of thanks. Invite everyone to bring their prayer to stick onto a map of the world (or a globe). You could show the images of human emotions from the **Bible talk** while this is being done.

Prayers of intercession
Explain that 'Hallelu hallelujah – praise ye the Lord' is known globally and ask if church members know this phrase in other languages. For example, in Bulgarian, it is: 'Hallelu hallelujah – slava na bog.'

It is appropriate to then pray for God's people across the world, including prayers for:
• Countries currently in the news and for specific situations
• Church mission partners with specific prayer for their work, context and family life
• Unity for the worldwide church and peace for this time of Christmas celebration

Between each section of prayers, the song 'Laudate omnes gentes' from Taizé (meaning 'Sing praises all you peoples/sing praises to the Lord') might be sung or played on a CD.

Ending the service

Show again the photos or PowerPoint slides used in the **Bible talk** which illustrate human emotions. Then encourage a short time of silent reflection and gratitude as people think about what they have discovered in the service in this season of Advent.

Helpful extras

Music and song ideas

'Shine Jesus shine' *SOF* 362
'Thine be the glory' *SOF* 551
'Tell out my soul' SOF 520
'Light for everyone' *LFE*
'Children of the world' *LFE*
'For God so loved the world' John Hardwick, *Action Packed Praise* DVD + CD and *34 Songs for All Occasions*
'The Word' *BSBS*, a Learn and remember verse song for John 1:14

A music score for 'Sing praises all you peoples' (Taizé) can be found on the weblink http://www.taize.fr/en_article464.html. A recording of the song is available on the CD, *Taizé: 'Laudate omnes gentes* and as a download on Amazon.

Notes and comments

Lighting an Advent wreath of candles is a great way to begin a service throughout Advent, especially as lighted candles play a part in this service. Explain that the four candles stand for a variety of things. One explanation is that each candle stands for people who proclaimed Jesus' birth – prophets, John the Baptist, angels and Mary – with the central candle standing for Jesus, which is lit on Christmas Day.

Make the most of the international flavour of this service, encouraging people from different national backgrounds to share what Advent means to them. Make sure that everyone is introduced to the mission partners who you may be praying for by showing photos and other information about them. Do not assume that everyone present will know them. With your refreshments, you could include some international foods, such as 'Lebkuchen', nachos, falafel, bruschetta or mini samosas.

Gifts galore

Nativity

Aim: to worship Jesus as Lord and King

Readings: Luke 1:26–38; 2:1–20; Matthew 1:18–25; 2:1–12

Getting started

Every year we encounter the Christmas story and it becomes so familiar that its awesome majesty can be lost. Of course, children are encountering the story for the first time at the age that they are, so it is not surprising that they are entranced by it, however much it has been wrapped up in the secular practices of Christmas. The challenge for any leader of an all-age nativity service is to allow the children to wonder, and to enable adults to 'see' the story with fresh eyes – and these days many adults themselves don't really know what happened.

In preparation, read the nativity accounts in both Matthew and Luke's gospels. As you do so, ask God to show you the many examples of generosity that there are in the story – the giving of time, effort, gifts, life plans, ambitions and, ultimately, the giving of a son.

During the course of this service a nativity tableau will be formed in an area clearly visible to a seated congregation. Ask adults and older children to take part, representing Mary, an angel, Joseph, three or four shepherds and three or four wise men. At the right time, they move into place, to stay as still as possible, thus creating a living picture of the nativity scene. Supply them with simple props and costumes. This will need rehearsing.

You will need

- Props and costumes for the actors and the tableau, including three labelled gifts (from the wise men) for the **Bible retelling** and **Bible talk**
- Sticky tape, scissors, wrapping paper and little 'gifts' for everyone (such as fun-sized chocolate or a satsuma) in the gift-wrapping 'stations'
- A wordsearch (AASA4.Nat_1) for **Beginning the service**
- People to lead the **Prayers of intercession**
- A copy of the prayer (AASA4.Nat_2) for **Ending the service**
- An Advent wreath and lighter (optional)

All downloads are freely available from www.scriptureunion.org.uk/lightdownloads.

Beginning the service

Before the service, set up the tableau 'furniture' with a stool near the manger lit by a spotlight. Just before the service, someone fills the manger with straw, fusses around as though in preparation, and then covers both stool and manger with a large blue and a large white cloth (or sheet). You could also display an image on the screen of a nativity scene.

Welcome everyone, then invite them to wrap up a gift at one of the wrapping 'stations'. Play Christmas music while this is happening. You could provide a wordsearch and pencils or a picture to colour if this is going to take long. A wordsearch (AASA4.Nat_1) is available.

When everyone is finally seated, welcome them and ask how many nativity plays the children have joined in during their life. Then ask how many the adults have participated in. Do a quick calculation to find the total number! This story is the beginning of the most important story ever. We can never tire of hearing it. This time we are all going to hear it, see it and take part in it in different ways!

Bible retelling

With: Four readers using a modern version of the Bible; props and actors for the tableau; song words and musicians

The following Bible readings are interspersed with songs and some comments, while the actors take their place in the tableau.

A long time ago…
Sing: 'Once in royal David's city'
(*Tableau: During the singing of verse 1, Mary moves to her place, picks up the blue cloth and wraps it around her as a cloak, then sits some distance from the manger. Wrapped in the white sheet over the shoulders, the angel stands nearby.*)

After the carol, lower the main lights, leaving the spotlight focused on the nativity scene.

Reader 1: Luke 1:26–38

A child is born
Ask the children what happens next? Fill in the story to the point where Mary and Joseph are in Bethlehem, there is nowhere for them to rest and Jesus is born.

Sing: 'Away in a manger'

(*Tableau: During the carol, Joseph joins the tableau and places the 'baby' in the manger while Mary moves her stool close to the manger. Joseph stands by her and both look at the manger.*)

Reader 2: Luke 2:1–7

Good news
Reader 3: Luke 2:8–20

Sing: 'While shepherds watched'
(*Tableau: During the carol, the shepherds move into their places in the tableau.*)

A very special baby
Comment on the shepherds' arrival. Ask the children about the nativity story. What gifts might the shepherds have brought for the baby? Who is missing from the nativity scene? (The wise men, of course!) Explain that it was probably some time after Jesus was born that these eastern visitors followed the star and found Jesus.

Sing: 'In the bleak midwinter'
(*Tableau: During the carol, the wise men bring their gifts, placing them so that they are visible to the audience at the front of the 'stage', and they join the scene.*)

Reader 4: Matthew 2:1–12

If possible, the actors should remain in position but if they are weary or wriggling, they can sit down. However, they will need to get back into position for the response in the **Prayer activity,** when the tableau is reassembled.

Bible talk

With: three gift boxes labelled 'Gold', 'Frankincense' and 'Myrrh' (with additional phrases – see below), laid at the front of the tableau, brought by the wise men; Isaiah 60:1–3 (CEV)

Ask the children what gifts they might give a new baby today. Say that Jesus was just like any other baby. He cried, made a mess in his nappy, kept his parents awake at night, slept, cooed and gurgled. But he was also a baby who was different, as seen by the announcements that were made about his birth, and also the gifts that he was given.

Comment on the different things that people gave in the story:

- Gabriel arrived to see Mary. Mary was all set to marry Joseph and expecting life to be pretty normal. She gave that up and **gave** herself to God, to do what he asked of her. Read Luke 1:38 again.
- This was all part of God's plan to make it possible for all people to be at peace in their relationship with God and with others. God **gave** his one and only son. Read John 3:16.
- The shepherds rushed to see what had happened in Bethlehem once the angels had told them about it. We don't actually know what the shepherds gave to Jesus and his parents, but we know that as they went back to work, they **gave** praises to God. Read Luke 2:20.
- The wise men also **gave** their special gifts. Invite everyone to now consider the three gifts.

Ask one child to pick up one of the three gifts from the tableau. Ask them to read aloud what is written on the label. Ask them what this was and why they think it was given to Jesus. Then talk about the gift. Repeat this with two more volunteers. You could be flexible in the order of the gifts.

Gold: Jesus is a King, a Ruler and Lord.
Frankincense: This was used by priests in worship of God and showed that Jesus is a Priest who came to help us know God. Incense also speaks of the holiness of God.
Myrrh: This was used in the burial customs of the time and pointed to the death of Jesus.

Explain that whilst we enjoy hearing this story, it is not just a nice story. Talk about how the story of Jesus' birth challenges us.

Gold: Will we let Jesus, as God's Son, rule in our lives, helping us to live God's way?
Frankincense: Jesus, as a Priest, made it possible for us to speak with God. How well do we want to communicate with God?
Myrrh: Jesus gave his life for us when he died on the cross. How can we show our gratitude to him for doing this for us?

Conclude by pointing out that God has given so much for us, and in response we can give ourselves to him, as we ask him to come to live within us. With God's help, we can go on giving praise to him and giving to others.

Prayer activity

Ask everyone to think about what Jesus (King, Priest and Saviour) means to them. Ask everyone to hold the gift they wrapped earlier as they think about how the story of Jesus' birth challenges them. What do they want to thank God for? Their gift can represent that.

During the singing of a carol, they can bring their gift to the manger in the tableau as a sign of their own worship of Jesus. These gifts can be distributed at the end of the service so, in one sense, people are also giving to others.

Prayers of intercession

Many people serve others at Christmas time. It would therefore be appropriate to pray for the following topics, asking a few people to prepare their prayers beforehand. Between each topic everyone could join in with the response based on 2 Corinthians 8:9:
Leader: Jesus gave up all his riches in heaven
Everyone: He became poor so that we could become rich.

- For people who will be giving of their time during Christmas; those who have to work, those who will be involved in Crisis at Christmas (or similar) and those who are preparing food for visitors.
- For people across the world who will not be receiving love or care from anyone this Christmas; in war zones, those orphaned or sick, those in areas of famine and drought.
- For everyone present, that we will be generous in our praise of God and our gifts to others.

Ending the service

Conclude with a carol such as 'O come, all ye faithful' or a similar carol of praise and worship. Then say the following prayer together (AASA4. Nat_2), also available as a download:

Father God, you gave your Son.
Jesus Christ, you gave your life.
Holy Spirit, you give us life.
Father, Son and Spirit, may we give our lives to you.
And so, may we give generously to others.
Amen.

Keep the tableau in place until the congregation is moving around. Then ask the actors to give out the wrapped gifts that have been placed in or near the manger, ensuring that everyone has a gift.

Make sure that everyone knows what other Christmas events and worship services are planned during the season of Christmas.

Helpful extras

Music and song ideas

Christmas Praise (HarperCollins*Publishers*) is a refreshing collection of carols and Christmas songs, to be used with all ages. Try to ensure that the carols and songs in this service are sufficiently traditional and child friendly, but possibly introduce one new one.

Suggested songs are: 'Once in royal' *SOF* 438
'Away in a manger' *SOF* 36
'While shepherds watched' *SOF* 602
'In the bleak midwinter' *SOF* 243
'O come all ye faithful' *SOF* 408

Notes and comments

Lighting an Advent wreath of candles is a great way to begin a service throughout Advent (see service 3).

A lot of preparation is needed to set this service up, with actors, props and the necessary rehearsal (which need not take long). Allow enough time in the preparation. There are lots of opportunities for people to get involved. Choose people to read the Bible who are good readers, using a version(s) of the Bible that is refreshing. At least one reading could be read by a cast of people, a narrator plus the relevant characters. Readers also need to practise.

For more ideas on presenting Christmas in a fresh way with quizzes, games, puzzles, assembly outlines, drama scripts and retold stories, visit lightlive.org or get hold of a copy of *Christmas Wrapped Up* or *More Christmas Wrapped Up* (SU). This service is a revised version of the nativity service for all ages from *Light 2006*.

The Lord is my shepherd

January

Light series: In God's hands
Light readings: Psalm 23; 1 Samuel 16:1−13; 17:1 − 18:5; 19; 20; 24

Aims: to explore this well known psalm in a multisensory way
to recognise that God is a shepherd, a protector and a provider
of good gifts

Readings: Psalm 23; John 10:14−16

Getting started

This month's *Light* series explores how, by putting his trust in God's Word, David the shepherd-boy, poet and musician became a man of action – a giant-slayer and brave warrior – who would one day be Israel's greatest king. He discovered that in God's hands we are safe, and can face our greatest fears. God loves each of us as we are and sees our full potential. If we trust in him we can begin to discover his protection, provision and guidance for ourselves, just as young David did.

Life in the twenty-first century is full of noise and activity. Our children have never known a world without mobile phones or computers. Many of us suffer from 'infobesity'! In this all-age service, we're not just sharing information about God: we're aiming to create a calm, quiet space where everyone can learn about David's famous prayer in an experiential way, meet with God themselves and respond by welcoming the Good Shepherd. This multi-sensory, reflective approach will come naturally to children who are used to using their imaginations; adults may need more help and encouragement to engage in this way, but may find that they end up seeing a familiar psalm in a whole new light.

You will need

- a projected image or illustration of 'Christmas card' shepherds (AASA4.Jan_2); two volunteers (one child to dress up, one youth/adult to assist); dressing up clothes and props; a projected or printed version of John 10:14−16 (CEV) (AASA4.Jan_3) for **Beginning the service** and for **Ending the service**
- three volunteers for the **Bible reading**, each with a 'script' (AASA4.Jan_1), having practised reading slowly and clearly
- walking stick or shepherd's crook; a shield; a tin of biscuits/box of sweets; someone primed to give a testimony for the **Bible talk**
- flipchart/OHP and pens; printed copies of Psalm 23 (or Bibles); paper and pens for the **Prayer activity**
- pens; pre-cut paper 'shields' (a template is at AASA4.Jan_5) for everyone for **Prayers of intercession**

All downloads are freely available from www.scriptureunion.org.uk/lightdownloads.

Beginning the service

With: a projected image of a traditional Christmas card depicting shepherds (AASA4.Jan_2) or a suitable card, photocopied onto acetate for an OHP or scanned into a PC; two volunteers (one to dress up and the other to assist); a nativity-style shepherd's costume; a shepherd's crook or walking stick; a catapult or home-made sling (a hammock-shaped piece of thick fabric with either end plaited – see *The 10 Must-Know Stories* (SU), 'The Secret Weapon', for an illustration (AASA4.Jan_4)); a cuddly toy lamb; a projected or printed version of John 10:14–16 (AASA4.Jan_3)

While the assistant dresses the volunteer as a shepherd, draw attention to the Christmas card image on the screen. Last month you would have been hearing about shepherds visiting baby Jesus. In those days, most people didn't think much of shepherds, but God chose them to be among the very first witnesses of his Son's birth. Shepherds are mentioned all the way through the Bible: Moses, the prophet Amos, David. Some, like David, even became kings! As an adult, Jesus would describe himself as 'The Good Shepherd', who knows his sheep and lays down his life for them.

Divide the church into two halves and get them to read alternate phrases of John 10:14–16, either projected onto the screen or in a printed version. This is what Jesus said about himself.

As the assistant finally hands the crook and sling to the volunteer, point out that in Bible times these were the tools of a shepherd's trade. A shepherd's crook, 'staff' or 'rod' helped him walk long distances up rocky paths and into the hills where the best grass grew. It could also be used to 'hook' a lamb if it started wandering off, and to pull it back onto the path. The sling, a bit like a catapult, was a weapon for firing stones at wild animals to stop them attacking the sheep.

Ask the congregation, 'if the volunteer really were a shepherd from Bible times, what do you think his or her new year's resolution would be?' Hopefully, you'll get answers such as: keep a close eye on the sheep so they don't wander off and get lost; practise with their sling till they're a really good shot and can protect the sheep; take the sheep to the best places to eat and drink; count the sheep without falling asleep!

Bible retelling

Ask two volunteers (A and B) to prepare Psalm 23 in the web version (AASA4.Jan_1), leaving a pause at every full stop and a longer pause at the end of each section. Introduce a third volunteer as the narrator who'll guide the congregation through a Bible meditation. Encourage everyone during the pauses to ask themselves what God might be saying to them through his Word.

Explain that this psalm was probably written by David, a shepherd boy who became Israel's greatest king. When he wrote this song, he was imagining God looking after him in the same way a shepherd looks after his sheep: leading him, protecting him and finding him food and drink.

Now read Psalm 23. Then allow a few more moments for quiet, prayerful reflection.

If you wish to use the Learn and remember verse (Psalm 59:9), this would be a good place to introduce it. It will be particularly encouraging for people who identified with Psalm 23:4. A song format is available online and in *Bitesize Bible Songs 2* (see **Music and song ideas**). Sing it together as an expression of faith to God who is our shepherd, protector and provider.

Bible talk

With: shepherd's crook; shield (or you could make one out of cardboard); tin of Christmas biscuits or sweets; a person with a personal story about their experience of God as shepherd, protector or provider

This talk is in three sections, following the pattern of the Bible meditation. In each section we explore a different aspect of God's love, each beginning with the letter string 'Sh'.

The Lord is my <u>Sh</u>epherd (Psalm 23:1–3) Hold up the shepherd's crook. Can people remember what it's for? The shepherd uses it when leading the sheep to good pasture, and to hook a lamb and pull it back if it's going off the path.

We need to know the Lord as our shepherd when we're tired and weary and when we've lost the feeling of well-being and contentment that comes from companionship, refreshing sleep or a good meal. We can look to God to give us what we need and help us feel better.

We need to know the Lord as our shepherd when we're not sure which way to go. Sometimes we have to make important choices like who to be friends with, whether or not to do something, what subjects to study, what job to do and where to live. We can ask Jesus to show us the best path for us to follow.
If we know we've wandered from God's ways like silly sheep and need rescuing, we can cry out to him to forgive us and 'hook' us back onto the path.

The Lord is my **Sh**ield (verse 4)
Hold up the shield. Who knows how to use a shield? Police officers sometimes hold shields in front of them to protect themselves when facing an angry crowd.

We need to know the Lord as our shield when we are in danger or afraid. When we go through difficult or sad, dark times we can remind ourselves that Jesus is with us, beside us, within us, before us and behind us – much better than a shield – more like a force field! He can protect us as we pray by helping us to stay calm, not to panic, and to think clearly as we try to listen to him and not our fears. David experienced this peace and protection from God when he risked his life for his country and fought the great warrior, Goliath.

The Lord **Sh**ares his good gifts (verses 5,6)
Hold up the biscuits/sweets. Ask what they think you've brought these for. Say they're a leftover Christmas present which you want to share with everyone after the service, so you can remind yourselves that God shares his good gifts with us.

We need to know this especially when things are not going so well for us. Perhaps we're aware of people who've hurt us or fought against us. Perhaps we don't know how we're going to pay the Christmas bills. Perhaps we realise we've failed God – or hurt someone – and don't know how we can be forgiven. But God's kindness and love are always with us. He pursues us to bless us. He doesn't give up. And the best gift of all was *Jesus*, the Good Shepherd. He gave up his life for us when he died on the cross so that we could find our way back to God, through him. (Remind people of the reading from John 10:14–16.)

To conclude, ask someone to (briefly) share a personal experience about a time when they knew God guiding them, keeping them safe, or treating them in a special way. You might interview them: What was the occasion? The danger? The need? The gift that God gave? What was their response? Were they filled with joy and praise like David was?

Recap the three main points, tying in the testimony you've just heard. What difference can it make to our lives knowing Jesus, the Good Shepherd?

Prayer activity
With: flipchart/OHP and suitable pens; printed copies of Psalm 23 for reference, or Bibles open on the right page

Explain that David was a musician and wrote lots of songs like Psalm 23 to praise God and to express his feelings, being happy, sad or frightened. God loves to listen to our thoughts and feelings. Look at some questions together and share ideas as you write your own church psalms. Encourage people to speak out: How are you feeling today? What do you want to tell God about? Do you want to ask him for his help? Have you had an answered prayer to thank him for? David thinks of God as a shepherd, or the host at a feast, or a 'refuge' and 'shield'. How else could you describe God?

Write down people's responses on the flipchart or OHP. If possible, group the ideas into verses, perhaps with a repeating refrain, if a theme emerges. The refrain could be Psalm 59:9b: 'You are my refuge, O God'. This psalm needn't rhyme or scan, but it will be a true expression of the emotions of the gathered church at this stage of their spiritual journey. To finish, read it aloud with everyone joining in with the refrain and 'Amen' at the end.

If there's someone who'd like to take it away and set it to music, this psalm could be used in your worship on another day!

Prayers of intercession
With: pens; pre-cut paper 'shields' (template at AASA4.Jan_5)

Remind people of David's 'dark valley' and how he was able to trust God and not be afraid even during hard times. Ask everyone to think of someone who might feel they're in a 'dark valley' because they're sad or facing problems like bullying, illness or big changes. Does this person need to know God as their **sh**epherd – guiding them; as a **sh**ield – protecting them; or the one who **sh**ares his good gifts with them – providing for them?

Give everyone a pen and a paper 'shield'. Ask them to write on it the name of the person they want to pray for and write or draw a picture to show what they need – a shepherd's crook, a shield, or a wrapped present. At a given sign, encourage people to read out loud the names they've written. Draw the prayer time to a close with a 'cover-all' prayer. Encourage everyone to take home their prayer shields and remember to keep praying.

Ending the service

With: projected Bible text John 10:14–16 (CEV) and the image of the Christmas card shepherds from **Beginning the service**

Project John 10:14–16 again on the screen (or use Bibles or printed copies) and read aloud, prefacing the reading with 'Jesus said:' then revert to the projected image of the Christmas card shepherds and lead everyone in the following prayer:
We thank you, Lord, that you are our shepherd, our shield and the one who shares good gifts with us. We praise you for the best gift of all, your Son Jesus, who gave up his life for us. This is such good news that we can't keep it to ourselves! Help us, Lord, to go out and find the people who don't yet know your love, and to invite them to join us in your 'flock'.

Helpful extras

Music and song ideas

'Blessed be the name of the Lord' *SOF* 673
'He brought me to his banqueting table' *SOF* 750
'Shout for joy and sing' *SOF* 496
'The Lord's my shepherd' *SOF* 1030 or another song version of Psalm 23
'UR my refuge' *BSBS2*, a Learn and remember song for Psalm 59:9

Notes and comments

If the church is going through a particularly dark valley corporately, as a **Prayer activity** you could create a 'prayer wall' with everyone's names on it. Cut out a giant 'shield' shape and ask everyone to either write their name or draw a picture of themselves on the shield. Add your church's name and these words based on Psalm 23:4 as the motto, 'We won't be afraid. You are with us.'

The midweek club material in *Target Challenge* (SU) contains lots more ideas on engaging with this psalm and the younger life of David. Look for ways of connecting with the rest of the *Light* series on David.

Have a read of this!

February

Light series: Illustrated letters
Light readings: Philippians 2:25−30; Philemon; 2 Timothy 1:3−10; 3:14−17

Aims: to explore one of Paul's letters as he communicated his desire to see people grow in faith
to identify how people of all ages can help others to grow spiritually

Readings: Philippians 1:12−20; Ruth 1:1−22

Getting started

The *Light* series looks at some of Paul's letters, including Philippians. In this service we look at a few verses from Philippians, to see how Paul worked. All his letters are written to particular situations in the first century, to real people who were encountering specific problems in the church. This accounts for the very different subjects he writes about and the way that they are written.

Philippi was the first place Paul visited when he came into Macedonia, the northern part of Greece (Acts 16:11−40). The first converts were a rich businesswoman and a rough Roman jailer! Paul himself is in prison by the time he writes to them, or under house arrest, probably in Rome (Acts 28:17−31). He encourages these Christians to keep Jesus at the centre of their lives, living in ways that please Christ and show his love to the world.

In Philippians 1:12−20 Paul is encouraged that, despite his imprisonment, the good news of Jesus is being shared with others. His first thoughts are not for his own safety but for them. He wants to be sure that they are getting to know God better and are supporting and encouraging each other.

The reading from Ruth shows how Ruth's commitment to Naomi opened the way for both of them to grow in faith.

You will need

- Human bingo sheets (AASA4.Feb_3) for **Beginning the service** or the **Game**
- Bible readers and people prepared to talk about answers to prayer in the **Bible talk**
- Cards with the Bible passages (AASA4.Feb_1 − Card 1: Philippians 1:3−6; Card 2: Philippians 2:1−4; Card 3: Philippians 3:12−14,17; Card 4: Philippians 4:8,9,13)
- Headings to display; two Post-it notes; pens; a small pebble for each person; a picture or drawing of the church for the **Bible talk** and **Prayer response**
- Bookmarks of prayer requests for the church family for **Ending the service**

All downloads are freely available from www.scriptureunion.org.uk/lightdownloads.

Beginning the service

With: optional sheets for human bingo

Thinking about the nature of the church and the way that we relate to one another, it would be good to start by focusing on the church. This could be done by singing a hymn like 'The church's one foundation', using the notices to draw attention to the life of the church or encouraging people to talk to one another, especially those they don't know well.

For a more interactive option use the **Game**, human bingo.

Bible reading

The person reading Philippians 1:12–20 could dress up in roughly first century clothing and read as though this is their personal letter to the people listening.

Ruth 1:1–22 could be dramatised with three people, possibly in appropriate costume, coming down the aisle to play the parts of Naomi, Ruth, and Orpah (who has no words to say). A narrator will also be required. (This reading will be repeated in Service outline 8, for Mothering Sunday.)

Bible talk

With: headings (see below) on pieces of card to display or on a PowerPoint; Bible verses (CEV version AASA4.Feb_1) on four cards placed around the church; people prepared to speak about answers to prayer or sports training; pebbles; Post-it notes (ideally arrow-shaped ones as a sign of being active); large picture of the church; pens

The talk is based around four small parts of Paul's letter to the Philippians. These passages should be printed out on postcards and hidden around the church. It would be best to number them. Ask children to find them and bring them to the front where they can read them out loud. (Younger children will need help with the reading but not with the 'finding'.) Talk about each one as suggested below. Alternatively, distribute the passages among small groups in the congregation (family groups if appropriate). Ask them to list the things that Paul is thinking and writing about. Take feedback and then summarise.

This talk could be given in two ways. The suggestion here is to divide the **Bible talk** into four sections each followed by a **Prayer activity** to encourage response to what has been said. Alternatively, present the talk in one or two sections and choose which response ideas are most suitable.

When Paul wrote this letter he was either in prison or under house arrest. He would not have been able to go out and he was chained to a Roman soldier. How would we feel about being in prison? Invite as many different suggestions as possible. Write them up on a flip chart, OHP or data projector. Then ask what we would be thinking about most if we were in prison. Again encourage as many contributions as possible and record them.

In this **Bible talk**, we will look at one letter that Paul wrote to see how he felt and what he was thinking about. There is not enough time to look at the whole letter, so we will just look at four sections. Give some background on where Philippi is and how the church got started (see Acts 16).

Pray for one another

Ask the person who has Card 1 to bring it up and read out Philippians 1:3–6.

Paul is thinking not about himself but about the Christians in Philippi. We might expect him to be worried about his own future, but he is more concerned that God will carry on with what he has started to do in the lives of the Philippians. He is always thinking about others. He wants them to know God better.

One of the ways that we can help others to know God better and to live as he wants is to pray for them. Depending on the nature and age of the congregation, point out that much of our prayer for others happens at times of crisis and is about specific physical needs or situations. Paul prays for the spiritual welfare and development of these Christians, who are not necessarily in a crisis. If appropriate, include one personal story from someone about answered prayer, not forgetting that stories from children about answered prayer are often the most powerful and encouraging.

What does Paul want them to do? He wants them to pray for one another. Stick up the large card with the words: Pray for one another.

Prayer response

Give each person a small pebble. Ask them to

think of someone else in the church and what they would like God to do for this person. Then ask them to bring the pebble and place it in a basket as an act of prayer for that person. A more complex alternative would be to ask them to write the name of the person and the request on the pebble with a felt-tip pen. When all the pebbles have been brought to the front, use the following prayer based on Philippians 1:9–11:

May our love for God and for one another keep on growing,
May we fully know and understand how to make the right choices,
May we be kept pure and innocent until Jesus comes back.
May Jesus keep us busy doing good deeds that bring glory and praise to God.

Care for one another
Ask someone to bring up Card 2 (Philippians 2:1–4) and read it out. One of the things that Paul wants for the Christians in Philippi is for them to get on well together. They are not to fight and argue but to support and care for each other. When we are more interested in what *we* want than in what *others* need we are not doing what God wants. Only when we look out for the needs of others and do things for them, rather than just looking after ourselves, can we expect to grow as a church.

If you have read the story of Ruth and Naomi, comment that this is a wonderful example of what it means to care for one another and put other people's needs before our own.

Put up the card saying: Care for one another.

Prayer response
Ask everyone to think of someone they could help in some way this week. They should make a practical plan and write it down on one of their Post-it notes and then place it in their Bible or pocket as a reminder. Family groups could work together. Conclude by praying that God will help us to care for one another.

Encourage one another
Someone brings up Card 3 and reads Philippians 3:12–14,17. Paul knew that he wasn't perfect. He still had a lot to learn and wanted to be able to serve God better. All of his energy went into making that happen. He was like a runner straining every muscle to reach the finishing line. He encouraged the Philippians to follow his example, to keep going, to keep 'training' to be

as close to God as possible. If there is anyone in the church who is involved in a sport, ask them to talk about their training regime, especially emphasising the role which others play in encouraging and supporting them.

Put up the third heading: Encourage one another.

Prayer response
Display a large picture, photo or diagram of the church. On the second Post-it note ask everyone to write a message of encouragement for someone or a group in the church. Younger children might draw someone they care about. They should then stick these on the large picture. Leave these so that they can be read at the end of the service.

Focus on Jesus and rely on God
Finally ask the person with Card 4 to come to read Philippians 4:8,9,13. All the way through this letter Paul is focused on Jesus (see for example 1:21; 2:5–11, but there are references to Jesus all through the letter). Every day our minds are filled with images from the TV screen, advertising and what we see in our world or in our street. We need to be careful about what we give our attention to. Thinking about things that are right and good helps us to grow in our relationship with God. The best way to do this is to think about Jesus, what he has done and the sort of person he was. We want to be like him and to encourage others to do the same. God will give us the strength that we need to do this.

Stick up the final heading: Focus on Jesus and rely on God.

Prayer response
Join together in this prayer based on Philippians 2:6–11 (AASA4.Feb_2).

Lord Jesus, we praise you because
Although you are truly God,
You did not try to remain
equal with God.
Instead you gave up everything
and became a slave,
and became
like one of us.
You were humble,
You obeyed God and even died
on a cross.
We praise you because God has given you
the highest place,
and honoured your name
above all others.

So that at your name
everyone will bow down,
those in heaven, on earth,
and under the earth.
And to the glory
of God the Father,
everyone will openly agree,
'Jesus Christ is Lord!'

We ask you to keep
our thoughts fixed on you,
And to make
our love for you strong,
And to help us to
live as you want us to.

based on Philippians 2:6–11

Ending the service

With: bookmarks of prayer ideas for the church family

Run through the headings which describe Paul's own practice and his instructions to the Christians in Philippi. Encourage everyone to put what they have learnt into practice.

Close with this blessing based on Philippians 1:6:

And now may the God who has begun a good work in our lives carry on his work through this next week, so that one day it will be finished.

Give everyone a bookmark as they leave.

Helpful extras

Music and song ideas

'The church's one foundation' *SOF* 525
'How deep the Father's love for us' *SOF* 780
'God's people aren't super brave' ks 86
'God loves and I love you' ks 80
'You are the vine' *SOF* 629
'My grace' *BSBS2* which is a Learn and remember verse song for 2 Corinthians 12:9
'Climb on, climb up high' *LFE*

Game

With: sheets for human bingo (AASA4.Feb_3)

In advance, you will need to find out certain facts about the congregation. These could relate to where they live, what car they drive, how many are in their family and so on. The sample downloadable sheet gives the idea, along with a blank template. It would be possible to include more boxes but nine is probably more than enough for an all-age service.

The idea is simple. Everyone is given a 'human bingo sheet' and a pen. In a short space of time they find someone who fits each category, putting the name of this person in the relevant box. It is best to let the game run for a fixed period of time. Young children will need an adult helper, as will any who are less mobile or visiting.

Notes and comments

The story of Ruth is the focus of Service 8, for Mothering Sunday.

Getting to grips with Paul's letters is quite complex and leaders of the children's groups may have found this *Light* series 'Illustrated letters' a challenge. This all-age service outline plays an important part in laying foundations or drawing the series together, depending on when the service falls. Obviously the outline is self-standing. Do make sure that everyone (adults and children) knows something of the background of Paul's life and mission.

Accept or reject?

March

Light series: Jesus challenges us
Light readings: Matthew 7:13–29; 25:1–13; 25:14–30; 25:31–46

Aims: to see how Jesus revealed who he was, which people chose to accept or reject
to examine how we welcome Jesus

Readings: Matthew 21:33–46; Isaiah 53:3–6

Getting started

The focus of *Light* this month is on how Jesus challenges us. Matthew 7:13–29 provides the challenge to bear good fruit and to build life on the rock by listening to Jesus and living as he wants. Matthew 25:1–13 contains the challenge to be ready to welcome Jesus while verses14–30 call people to show love for Jesus by sharing with others what he gives .The parable of the sheep and goats, in verses 31–46, explains that one day everyone will have to give an account of their lives to Jesus. In this service we face the challenge of deciding to accept or reject Jesus.

All of these challenges come in the context of Jesus' teaching on the signs of the end times, immediately prior to his arrest and trial. His death (and resurrection) would turn everything upside down. The rejection of the servant in Isaiah 53 ultimately offers hope to those who accept him.

The challenge of all-age worship is to present scripture in ways which will nourish the faith of all ages. The service needs to be led with enthusiasm while difficult language and concepts need to be explained and communicated with clarity.

You will need:

- rules of the game 'Paper, scissors and stone' from: http://en.wikipedia.org/wiki/Rock-paper-scissors for **Beginning the service**
- Matthew 21:33–46 CEV (AASA4.Mar_1) printed or on PowerPoint; optional costumes and props for the readers in the **Bible reading**
- ten pictures of things people either like or dislike, for the **Bible talk**
- rough stones, one for everyone (from garden centres) for **Prayer of confession**
- a flip chart and pen for **Prayers of intercession**

All downloads are freely available from www.scriptureunion.org.uk/lightdownloads.

Beginning the service

Play the game of 'Paper, scissors and stone (or rock)'. Clearly use the word 'challenge' when asking for volunteers to come forward to play the game. Play the best of three with the first volunteer. The winner then 'challenges' another person to come and play.

This service will pick up on the idea of 'challenge' later, which is why it's important to use the word as much as possible at this point. Explain that the aim of the service is to look at how Jesus challenged the religious leaders of his day to accept or reject him and to think about whether or not we accept or reject Jesus today.

Bible reading

Read Matthew 21:33–46 – you will need a narrator, Jesus, several people to be vineyard renters and the chief priests and leaders. Readers could wear something simple to signify their parts. Alternatively, divide up the congregation to play the different parts, each part reading in unison. If you do this, the Bible verses will need to be either printed or on a PowerPoint (AASA4.Mar_1).

Narrator: Jesus told the chief priests and leaders to listen to this story:

Jesus: A landowner once planted a vineyard. He built a wall around it and dug a pit to crush the grapes in. He also built a lookout tower. Then he rented out his vineyard and left the country. When it was harvest time, the owner sent some servants to get his share of the grapes. But the renters grabbed those servants. They beat up one, killed one, and stoned one of them to death.

Congregation: Booo (everyone boos the renters)

Jesus: He then sent more servants than he did the first time. But the renters treated them in the same way.

Congregation: Booo

Jesus: Finally, the owner sent his own son to the renters, because he thought they would respect him. But when they saw the man's son, they said,

---

Vineyard renters (in unison): Someday he will own the vineyard. Let's kill him! Then we can have it all for ourselves.

Jesus: So they grabbed him, threw him out of the vineyard, and killed him.

Congregation: Booo

Jesus: When the owner of that vineyard comes, what do you suppose he will do to those renters?

Chief Priests and Leaders: He will kill them in some horrible way. Then he will rent out his vineyard to people who will give him his share of grapes at harvest time.

Jesus: You surely know that the Scriptures say: 'The stone that the builders tossed aside is now the most important stone of all. This is something the Lord has done, and it is amazing to us.' I tell you that God's kingdom will be taken from you and given to people who will do what he demands. Anyone who stumbles over this stone will be crushed, and anyone it falls on will be smashed to pieces.

Narrator: When the chief priests and the Pharisees heard these stories, they knew that Jesus was talking about them. So they looked for a way to arrest Jesus. But they were afraid to, because the people thought he was a prophet.

Matthew 21:33–46 (CEV)

Before reading Isaiah 53:3–6, explain that the prophet was talking about God's servant being rejected. This may have been meaning God's people, Israel, but it certainly also applied to Jesus, God's Son, who was rejected.

Bible talk

With: hidden pictures of at least ten things people either like or dislike (such as homework, ironing, cake, birthday presents, the dentist, football, going on holiday); a colourful bucket; a melancholy sound such as a horn but it could be made with the human voice

Ask children in school years up to year 6 to go around the building looking for the hidden pictures, bringing them back to the front. Explain that you all have to decide whether to 'accept' or 'reject' each object, saying that to accept something means to say 'Yes' to it, while to reject something means to say 'No'. (This is a version of the television programme 'Room 101'. Make it as zany as you like in the spirit of the original programme!)

Ask the children to hold up their pictures in turn. For each picture first ask those who accept it to cheer, and then ask those who reject it to boo. The loudest noise determines what is accepted or rejected. A rejected object is dropped into the bucket with the negative sound. Accepted objects are held up until the end. When you have worked through all the objects, thank the children and ask them to sit down.

Go over the Bible story by asking a number of questions. Questions should be appropriate for different age groups with a mixture of factual ones and those searching for some interpretation. For example: Who did Jesus tell the story to?
What did the owner of the vineyard do? What happened to the servants when they went to get the owner's share of the grapes from the renters? What happened to the owner's son when he went to get the grapes? The stone that Jesus talked about in the story represented a person. Who was it? (Some children may be able to answer this.) What did Jesus say would happen to the chief priests and the leaders if they didn't accept Jesus? (This is quite a hard question.)

Jesus told this story as a challenge to the chief priests and leaders. Remind people what the word 'challenge' means by referring back to the game of 'Paper, scissors and stone' at **Beginning the service**.

The Old Testament reading in Isaiah 53 talked about God's servant being rejected. The chief priests and leaders would know this prophecy. Jesus was warning them that if they rejected his challenge to know him (if they said 'No') they wouldn't know God. It would be the people who accepted Jesus' challenge to know him (the ones who said 'Yes') who would know God.

Jesus presents us with the same challenge. Are we going to accept his challenge to know him? Are we going to say 'Yes' to Jesus? Or are we going to reject him and say 'No'? Remember that Jesus said that the kingdom of God belongs to those who say 'Yes' to him, who live as he wants them to live. Jesus welcomes us and wants us to know him. Today, let's be people who accept his

welcome and his challenge and who say 'Yes' to knowing him.

At this point, include a short story from a member of the congregation about how they accepted and said 'Yes' to Jesus' challenge to follow him. Follow this with the **Prayer of confession**.

Prayer of confession

With: rough stones; the bucket from **Beginning the service**

Give out the stones as people arrive but ask everyone to put their stone in a safe place until needed. Alternatively, distribute them during a song directly before the **Prayer of confession**.

This activity focuses on times when we reject (say 'No') to Jesus, or fail to live as he wants us to. Draw attention to the fact that one of the servants in the story was stoned. (Others were put to death in other ways.) The stone stands for doing things that displease God, that say 'No' to him. Ask everyone to be completely quiet for a short time as they think of what they want to say sorry to God for. (Children respond well to being asked to be completely quiet providing it's only for a brief time.)

Then ask people to bring their stone to the front and drop it into the bucket as a reminder of everything they want to say sorry to Jesus for. Whilst this is happening, either sing a suitable song or play quiet, thoughtful music. You could make the melancholic sound every time something goes into the bucket, as in Room 101. (Children would find this more fun and memorable!)

When everyone has brought their stone forward, read out Isaiah 53:5:

> Jesus was beaten so we could be whole.
> Jesus was whipped so we could be healed.
>
> Isaiah 53:5 (NLT)

This will remind people that God has forgiven them and made them whole.

Prayers of intercession

With: a flip chart with words of opposite characteristics of how we might live, such as good: bad; truthful: dishonest; kind: cruel (with the positive/God-like ones in one column and the others in a second column).

If there's time beforehand, ask some children to help you construct the list of characteristics. In small groups, identify activities (personal or in the wider world) that could be described in the positive or the negative ways, such as Truthful (owning up when we have done something wrong) or Lying (covering up for wrong things). You could ask for feedback.

Then ask everyone to stand up and say together:
Dear God, help us to say 'Yes' to being… (Kind).
Help us to say 'No' to being… (Cruel).

Go through the whole list on the flipchart in this way. You could then identify areas in the world where there is a clear need for people to choose to accept to live God's way, rejecting the alternatives. Repeat the prayer above.

Ending the service

With: the bucket from **Beginning the service**; a large polished stone

Jesus welcomes us all and calls us all to accept him. Shake the bucket as a reminder of all that has been rejected. Then hold up a large, attractive, polished stone. This stands for all that is pure and good and of God. This is what you are all challenged to accept.
Invite everyone to follow what you now say and do, doing it at least twice:
(*Hold your hands, palms outwards, covering your face and then thrust them outwards in an action of rejection.*) Say: We say 'No' to living in a way that displeases God. (The melancholic sound could be played each time this is said.)
(*Hold your hands in front of you, palms upwards, then draw them towards your face.*) Say: We say 'Yes' to living in a way that pleases God.
Lord Jesus, help us to accept your challenge this week. Amen

Helpful extras

Music and song ideas

'Lord have mercy' *SOF* 354
'All I once held dear' *SOF* 646 – note the reference in the chorus to 'Knowing you, Jesus'
'Kyrie Eleison, Christe Eleison' Taizé chant
'I will worship with all of my heart' *SOF* 859
– picks up on the theme of accepting Jesus;
'Will you come and follow me?' *SOF* 1120
'Christ is made the sure foundation' *SOF* 1199
'In Christ alone' *SOF* 1346
'You can have my whole life' *SOF* 1660
'You are' *BSBS2* a Learn and remember verse song for Psalm 119:137,138
'I try to do what's good' *RU*

Notes and comments

If the service includes a baptism or thanksgiving for a child, you could tailor the talk to refer to promises and commitments that the parents will be making to bring the child up to know Jesus, and the need for the parents to accept Jesus' challenge to follow him for themselves.

If the service includes Holy Communion, you could remind everyone of the suffering of God's servant in Isaiah 53.

Ruth – God's answer

Mothering Sunday

Light series: Ruth, the widow
Light readings: Ruth 1; 2–4

Aims: to hear the story of Ruth's love for Naomi, her mother-in-law
to show God's love to anyone who is like a mother or father to us

Readings: Ruth 1:1–22; 4:9–17; Isaiah 45:17

Getting started

This service accompanies a two-part *Light* series on Ruth, seeing how God provides for two women. Naomi and her husband, Elimelech, had gone to Moab, a country to the east of Israel, on the other side of the Dead Sea. The Moabites had had lots of dealings with the people of Israel (for example, Genesis 14:5; Judges 11:17) but were not worshippers of the God of Israel. Moab must have been spared the famine that afflicted Bethlehem.

Elimelech became part of the community but the tragedies of the death of all the men in the family prompted Naomi to return home. Ruth's commitment to her mother-in-law was remarkable in that she clearly had a choice to remain with her own family, with the expectation that she might marry again. Her choice did not lead to immediate satisfaction, but this is a story with a happy ending. She remains an example of care for those for whom people have responsibility. God demonstrates his care through such sacrificial action.

This service outline reviews (or introduces) the whole story with an appropriate emphasis on those who care for others. Since it is not an example of a mother caring for a child (quite the reverse), it provides material that speaks to anyone who cares, including children's care for parents, grandparents and others in need.

You will need:

- two sweet drinks and two sour/bitter ones for **Beginning the service**
- actors and actresses plus chairs and props for the **Bible reading** and **Bible talk**
- construction materials for the **Prayer activity**
- copy of the grid (AASA4.Mother_2) for the **Game**
- a copy of the prayer (AASA4.Mother_1) for **Ending the service**

All downloads are freely available from www.scriptureunion.org.uk/lightdownloads.

Beginning the service

With: two sweet drinks and two sour/bitter ones

Ask two children to taste the two drinks. What words would they use to describe them both? Life can sometimes be described as bitter and sometimes sweet and sometimes we put the two words together, saying something is both bitter and sweet. (Give a personal example of this if you can.)

The Bible story today is about two women who experienced much bitterness but also sweetness. The elder of them even asked to be called 'Bitter' (Mara). We will hear how the younger woman loved and supported the older one, and the way that God was able to bless them both, in the bitter and in the sweet times. (Alternatively, use the **Game** to make this point.)

Ask who the people are in church that others lean on. A roving mike could pick up names. The children will probably say their parents or grandparents. Explain that in this service, there is going to be a role reversal, as people are encouraged to support and love those whom they usually lean on.

Bible reading

With: six chairs facing the front, four on one side (on which are sitting three men (Elimelech, Mahlon, Chilion and one woman, Naomi) and two on the other side (on which are sat two women, Ruth and Orpah); a seventh chair is taken by Boaz for the reading in Ruth 4.

As Ruth 1 is read, the actors move their chairs as appropriate. The group of four move their chairs to go to Moab (verse 1).

Elimelech turns his chair back to the audience (verse 3), the sons sit next to their wives (verse 4) and then turn their chairs away, as they die (verse 5).

Naomi, Ruth and Orpah carry their chairs halfway to the other side (verse 6) but Orpah returns (verse 14) and Ruth and Naomi continue (verse 18,19), sitting glumly on their arrival (verse 20).

Reading Ruth 4:9–17, Boaz joins Naomi and Ruth but sits apart from them and mimes as he addresses the audience who are acting as the town leaders (verses 9–12).

Ruth moves her chair next to Boaz (verse 13), then Naomi joins Ruth and bounces an imaginary child on her knee (verse 14).

The *Testament* series of animated Bible stories (from S4c), includes a 25-minute telling of the story of Ruth. This is available from the Bible Society and would be an alternative means of not only telling the story but would reinforce what the children have been learning in their Sunday groups. You would need to modify the rest of the service in the light of this. Do see the whole film through before showing it in a church service to ensure it is suitable for the audience.

Bible talk

With: an actress; a heavy sack; two bags of flour

What did Ruth do to support and care for her mother-in-law, Naomi?

Ruth refused to let Naomi travel on her own

Remind everyone of how Naomi's husband and two sons had died, so she was all on her own in a foreign country. She decided to travel back to where she came from, a town called Bethlehem where King David was later to be born and where Jesus was also born.

Ruth (who had married one of Naomi's sons) could have stayed with her own family and she might have found another husband. But she chose to go with Naomi, on a long and tough journey, to a place she had never been to before, where she had no family (apart from Naomi) or friends and no certain future. Being a younger woman she probably carried a lot of their belongings which they took with them. (*The actress picks up a heavy rucksack and wearily carries it across the front of the church.*) This must have been very bitter for both Naomi and Ruth. (*Stick the word 'bitter' on the sack, once it is put down.*)

Ruth worked hard to get them some food

When they got to Bethlehem, people recognised Naomi and were amazed to see her come back. She asked to change her name from 'Naomi', which means 'pleasant' to 'Mara', which means 'bitter'. They settled down and Ruth went to pick up the remains of the grain left over by those gathering in the harvest – after all, they had no money and they had to eat something.

(The actress wearily walks across the front carrying two bags of flour.) Remind everyone that grain is ground into flour. Life must still have been bitter for them. *(Stick the word 'bitter' on the flour, once it is put down.)*

Ruth made Naomi happy

Ruth discovered that she had been collecting the leftover grain from a relative of Naomi. The relative, a man called Boaz, made sure that there was plenty of grain left for her to collect. In those days, relatives had to take care of members of their family if they did not have anyone else to care for them. Ruth challenged Boaz about his responsibility to care for her and Naomi.

The story ends with Boaz agreeing to marry Ruth, welcoming her more fully into his (and Naomi's) family. Ruth had a son called Obed but everyone called him 'Naomi's Boy' because she was so pleased to have a grandson! The Bible even says that Naomi took good care of him. Read Ruth 4:14,15 again at this point. *(The actress cheerfully walks across the front carrying a doll, unless there is suitable access to a baby. Stick the word 'sweet' on the doll as it passes or is put down.)*

Ruth had cared for her mother-in-law through the tough, bitter times. God cared for Naomi through Ruth in the tough times. He cared for them in the sweet times too.

How can we care for those who usually care for us, in the bitter and in the sweet times?

Prayer activity

There are two aspects to this: to thank God for those who care for us and to ask God to help us to care for our carers. There are several suggestions for things to make and do for carers, with children and adults working together as appropriate. Choose which best suits your situation.

Begin by thanking God for all those who care for us. Ask some children to prepare prayers of gratitude to God.

Then explain that everyone is going to make at least one thing to give to someone who cares for them. Here are some suggestions.

Planting a bulb

With: bulbs; plastic pots; compost; wooden lollipop sticks; pens; copies of the following

phrases – God cares for you; Trust in God; May God bless you; Thank you (these phrases could already be written on the sticks)

Plant a bulb in a pot and stick a lollipop stick into the pot. People could write their own message or a Bible verse on the stick.

As an alternative, if plants or flowers are to be given to mothers in the service (carers, women, any adults in church!), they could be personalised by a ribbon being wrapped around the flowers with a gift label attached, containing a message or Bible verse. People could write their own message on the label.

Card-making

With: A5 card; glue; scissors; heart shapes, slightly smaller than A6; glitter; pens

Fold the card in half (A6), glue all over the heart, then sprinkle glitter over it. When it has dried slightly, stick it on the front of the card. Inside, children and adults can write a message to the person they love, and include the phrase: 'God loves you' or 'God cares for you', (or this could already be printed inside the card).

This can be made far more complicated by providing colouring and glitter pens, creating lots of little hearts, using glitter hearts or tying ribbon around the fold of the card.

Potpourri bag

With: squares of fabric, potpourri, elastic bands, ribbon, gift labels

Place a handful of potpourri mixture in the centre of a square of pretty fabric (cutting with pinking shears will give an attractive edge) and close into a bag, sealing it with an elastic band. Tie a ribbon and gift label around the band. The label can be prepared beforehand and/or personalised – see above.

Prayer of confession

Both carers and those cared for can sometimes fail to care for each other. Remind people of this and allow a short time for people to ask God to forgive them for the times when they have been selfish.

Then read out Isaiah 45:17 to remind everyone that God's love for us is eternal. God cares for us in the bitter and sweet times.

Ending the service

Provide an opportunity for children and those cared for to give their gifts to those who care for them.

Everyone gathers together in small groups, making sure no one is excluded. Say the following prayer (AASA4.Mother_1) together:

Leader: We thank you, Father God, for your love for us.
Group 1: Thank you that your love goes on for ever.
Group 2: Thank you that you will never forget us.
Group 1: Thank you that you provide for us in so many ways.
Group 2: Thank you that we belong to you.
Leader: Help us all to learn to care for those who love us in the same way.
Amen

Helpful extras

Music and song ideas

'All my hope on God is founded' *MP* 16
'Great is thy faithfulness' *SOF* 147
'What a friend I've found' *SOF* 1109
'How deep the Father's love for us' *SOF* 780
'Faithful One, so unchanging' *SOF* 89
'The Lord's my shepherd' *SOF* 1030
'For the beauty of the earth' *SOF* 112

Game

The idea of bitter and sweet things could be developed into a game before the **Bible talk**. Create a 12-square grid of pictures (or the words) of three sweet and three bitter tasting foods, which will be shown twice on the grid. The foods could be lemons, limes, gooseberries, doughnuts, chocolate and cakes. Cover these up with squares of paper that fit exactly, then ask children to pair up the identical squares, removing the paper and then replacing them again until a match has been found. See how many goes this takes to complete.

Alternatively, the grid (AASA4.Mother_2) is available to display on the screen.

Talk about how all these bitter and sweet foods are tasty, not necessarily bad. In the story of Naomi and Ruth they were to discover that God cared for them in the bitter and the sweet times.

Notes and comments

Mothering Sunday can be a difficult time for many people, so be sensitive to your congregation's particular situations. When talking about families and family life, be careful not to make anyone feel excluded, particularly single people or childless couples. Be aware of anyone who has lost a parent or child recently, and perhaps include a special time to pray for them. This service includes the opportunity to support anyone who usually cares for others, which includes fathers and grandparents and others in the community.

Choose the items which are most suited to your situation in the **Prayer activity**, trying to involve all ages in the service, without aiming it exclusively at children. Remember that there may be visitors who don't usually attend church, so make your language accessible and welcoming.

The best time in the service to distribute the gifts would be after the **Prayer activity,** although some churches like to give out flowers or gifts earlier in the service. Children whose carer is not in church can take their gift home.

Some churches provide breakfast or lunch for the whole family to make a fuss for mothers and carers. If you are doing this, you might show the *Testament* film about Ruth during this time (see **Bible reading**). For more ideas see *Celebrations sorted!* (SU).

Passover for the 21ˢᵗ century

April/Easter

Light series: Great love, great rescue
Light readings: Matthew 21:1−17; 28

Aims: to celebrate what God has done for us in Jesus
to have a deeper appreciation of his sacrifice through the
context of Passover

Readings: Exodus 12:1−28; Luke 22:7−20

Getting started

The *Light* series this month explores how the Easter story shows us God's love as he rescues his
people. This service expands that exploration to look in greater depth at the Passover meal which
Jesus celebrated with his friends just before he died. As Jesus celebrated God's rescue of his people
from slavery in Egypt, he initiated the Lord's Supper, a dramatic model of what he was about to do in
making it possible for people to be rescued.

Easter is a fabulous time to celebrate all that God has done for us in Jesus. However, in Sunday groups
much of the context of Jesus' death is missed since Palm Sunday is followed the next Sunday with
the focus on the resurrection. This Easter service is a celebration which incorporates elements of
the Passover meal Jesus shared with his friends, at which he established what became known as the
Lord's Supper.

If possible, provide trays of the elements for groups of people to share as you tell the story. If your
building or seating arrangements cannot accommodate this, have elements on small trays to pass
along rows. Alternatively, set up a dining-room-style table covered by a traditional white cloth and
invite guests to try out the elements, perhaps projecting a video image of the table onto a screen for
everyone to see. The Last Supper lends itself to all-age participation as it engages with all the senses.

You will need:

* the necessary ingredients to enact the Last Supper and (optional) video camera, tripod and
projector for **Beginning the service** and **Bible talk**
* an outline of a person on paper, one per person; pens or pencils; Blu-tack; lining paper for **Prayers
of intercession**, plus optional information about forced labour
* normal bread for the **Prayer of confession**
* party poppers, streamers, blowers and hats for **Ending the service**

Beginning the service

With: food ingredients for the Last Supper placed in trays and hidden under seats (see **Bible talk**), two candles

Welcome everyone and explain that today you'll be celebrating the freedom Jesus' death brought us. In advance, hide the elements in suitable containers under people's chairs. Ask them to look for things which might help us celebrate and bring them to a table at the front to be placed in view.

Explain that this time of year is Passover, which is when Jews (then and now) celebrate God rescuing his people from being slaves in Egypt. For every year of his life, Jesus would have celebrated this festival. He would have looked forward to sharing what was to be his last Passover meal with his friends with mixed feelings. Through this meal, he shared something of the significance of his death in a way his followers would never forget.

Passover is usually celebrated in people's homes over a long meal. Today you will explore Passover through the elements you have collected in order to understand and celebrate the freedom we have because of what Jesus did for us. This is the message of Easter Day! Freedom was only truly available after Jesus had come alive again.

At this point, light the two candles and say a prayer thanking God for his presence with you. Ask him to bring to light more of what Jesus' death and resurrection means for us. You could do the bread finding and **Prayer of confession** at this point.

Bible reading

Exodus 12:1–28, or selected verses: 3, 6–8, 11–14, 17; Luke 22:7–20

Put both passages in their context before they are read. Challenge everyone to listen out for and respond to three things in the readings: to 'baa' when they hear the word 'lamb', to shout 'no yeast!' for the word 'bread', and for the word 'Passover', raise their right hand high in the air to make an arching movement from right to left, while they say the word 'Pass over'. Practise this then start the readings, allowing time for people to respond to the three words.

Bible talk

With: two white candles in candle sticks; a white cloth; ingredients: parsley or celery, salt, charoset (see recipe in **Notes and comments**), a cooked lamb shank bone stripped of all the meat, a hard-boiled egg, raw horseradish or romaine lettuce, red wine or grape juice, three 'matzah' (bread without yeast available in large supermarkets); plates; optional video camera, tripod and projector

Remind people that Jesus celebrated Passover just a few days before he was killed. It wouldn't have been his first Passover, but it would be the last one he shared with his friends, and the one at which he gave the symbols new significance.

Make sure the trays of elements for everyone are ready or invite people of different ages to come to share in the elements of the Passover as you tell the story. If necessary, using a video camera, project the images of what is on the table for everyone to see.

If you've already had the reading, remind everyone that Exodus 12 is the pause before the climax to the story of the exodus from Egypt. If the service structure allows, start the story as below, then have the **Bible reading** at the appropriate place in the story.

Explain how Jacob's family moved from Canaan to Egypt to escape the famine, and there they grew into a huge family, so large that the Egyptians were afraid of them and made them work hard as slaves.

Bitter herbs
Invite people to try the bitter herbs (raw horseradish or romaine lettuce) explaining that these represent the bitter lives the Israelites had when they were slaves in Egypt.

Charoset
Ask people to try out some of the charoset, and explain that this represents the mortar used by the Israelites as they worked as Pharaoh's slaves to build his cities.

Parsley
Pass around the parsley which should be dipped in the salt and eaten. Say that this represents the salty tears of the Israelites as they cried out to God to save them.

Wine drops
Say that God heard their cries and made a

plan to rescue them. Pharaoh, the king, was not keen on losing his slaves, so God sent plagues on Egypt. Ask the congregation if they can remember the plagues. As they mention one, repeat it so everyone can hear. As you say each one, get people to drip a drop of the wine or grape juice from a cup onto their plate, as tears of blood. This is to represent the suffering of the Egyptian people.

Bread

Either read Exodus 12 here or remind everyone that today's reading came just before God sent the final plague. God told his people to be ready to leave, which is why they made unleavened bread, bread without yeast, as they had no time for it to rise. The special bread Jews now use for Passover is called 'matzah' and it has no yeast at all in it. Invite people to try the bread.

Lamb bone and egg

Remind people of how the Israelites were told to kill a lamb and put its blood on the doorposts of their houses so that the angel of death would pass over them. In the Passover meal, both the lamb shank bone and the middle pieces of bread represent the lamb. The boiled egg represents mourning for the temple which had been destroyed. Pass these elements round for people to touch but not eat.

In Jesus' day, they still ate a lamb on this night. They were about to go on a long journey so needed all the strength they could get. Jesus knew that very soon he would be killed, just as the Passover lamb was killed. He knew that the shedding of his blood would mean that everyone could be 'passed over', that everyone could be rescued and made free to be friends with God.

That's exactly what happened to the Israelites. That night, the angel of death passed over their houses, but killed the firstborn in every other house. Then the Egyptians urged the people of Israel to leave. They even paid them to go. It wasn't the end of their adventures or their troubles, but it was the start of them being free, free to be God's people.

The Lord's Supper

As part of the Passover meal, four cups of wine are drunk and three pieces of 'matzah' (bread without yeast) are eaten. The middle piece of bread represents the lamb and is broken in two. There is still some disagreement among Jews as to why this is still done, but for Christians this 'lamb' (broken bread) also represents Jesus,

the Lamb of God, whose body was broken. It was as Jesus broke this piece of bread that he said, 'This is my body given for you; do this in remembrance of me' (Luke 22:19). In the same way, Jesus used one of the four cups of wine as he said, 'This cup is the new covenant in my blood, which is poured out for you' (Luke 22:20).

Draw the parallel between Passover and the Lord's Supper, and how they both were given by God to celebrate what he was about to do for his people for years to come. You might like to share bread and wine at this point, either in the same way as the other Passover elements, or in your traditional way.

Prayer of confession

With: pieces of bread broken into crumbs

At traditional Jewish Passovers, the evening always starts with a hunt for breadcrumbs, as no leaven bread should be in the house (Exodus 12:19).

Before the service starts, hide some pieces of bread around your building and have fun as people search for the bread. As they do this, encourage everyone to search their hearts for anything which might stop them coming into God's presence today and enjoying the freedom which Jesus gives us. You could adapt and use 1 Corinthians 5:7,8 as a prayer of confession, or use a less formal version such as:
Help us, God, to search our hearts and remove anything which might stop us living for you.

Prayers of intercession

With: an outline of a person on paper, one per person; pens or pencils; sticky tape; strong rope or lifebelt (used to rescue people in trouble in the mountains or in the water)

Many people are in need of rescuing, even though they are not slaves in the physical sense. Encourage people to call out ideas of things we can be slaves to, such as fear, poverty, drugs, illness, boredom and hopelessness. Give out the people outlines and invite people to write on the outline the name or initials of someone or a group of people whom they have thought of. Invite people to stick their person to the rope or lifebelt as a representation of them being part of a crowd being rescued by God.

In addition, you could gather information about forced labour and fair trade from organisations such as Tearfund to display as a stimulus for prayer.

Ending the service

Recall that, having celebrated Passover with his friends, Jesus went out to pray, was arrested, tried and put to death on a cross, but three days later came alive again. God's plan for saving his people was completed.

Ask people to spend a moment choosing one element of the Passover which strikes them most or helps them remember what Jesus' death means for them. Challenge them to try and remember next time they come into contact with those elements (bread, wine, egg, etc) to remember God's rescue of the Israelites from Egypt and how, through Jesus, he has also rescued us and given us freedom to be his people.

End with a series of celebratory songs, using party poppers, streamers, blowers and hats.

Helpful extras

Music and song ideas

'Led like a lamb' *SOF* 322
'Jesus Christ is risen today' *SOF* 285
'Thine be the glory' *SOF* 551
'Lord I lift your name on high' *SOF* 897
Salvation belongs to our God' *SOF* 992
'Living one' *BSBS2*
'So much' *BSBS2*
'Mighty Saviour' *BSBS2* the Learn and remember verse song for Luke 1:69.

Do include at least one traditional Easter hymn/ song for the benefit of any visitors.

Notes and comments

The Heavenly Party by Michele Guinness (Monarch) has a Christian version of a Passover meal you can celebrate with your whole church. It is a fun service taken over a long, delicious meal.

Charoset recipe: Chop three apples and one cup of walnuts. Mix this with two teaspoons of cinnamon, 5 tablespoons of wine and one tablespoon of honey, and chill.

Children joining in this Passover demonstration are not necessarily joining in a service of Holy Communion. But do ensure that the church leadership finds this acceptable. It would be appropriate to incorporate elements of this service into an Easter celebration of Holy Communion.

Come close to God

May

Light series: Good King David?
Light readings: 2 Samuel 5:4–12; 6:1–19; 7; 9; 11:1 – 12:15

Aims: to hear about David's life, as a songwriter and to see this psalm
against the probable background of Absalom claiming the throne
to explore what it means to be close to God in adversity

Readings: Psalm 63 (2 Samuel 15–18); James 4:7,8

Getting started

The *Light* series has been exploring David's life as King of all Israel. (He was king of Judah for seven years, based in Hebron, before becoming king of the northern kingdom as well.) This builds on the outline in January based on David's early life (see Service 5). You will probably want to refer back to this and to Psalm 23 in particular.

Tradition has it that David wrote Psalm 63 while he was in exile from Jerusalem. The story of how Absalom usurped his father is a dramatic one, so do read 2 Samuel 15–18 as you prepare for this service. David had good cause to use desert imagery in describing his longing and thirsting for God (verse 1). It was a time for remembering (verses 2,6). As a poet he used imagery to describe his relationship with God (singing in the shadow of God's wings, held by God's powerful arm), ending on a note of hope and justice! James' call to come close to God (4:7,8) is accompanied by a call to holy living.

May everyone in this service experience God's closeness and confident hope whatever the adversity! This is clearly relevant for all ages.

You will need
- Images or mime for the **Bible reading**
- Flip chart, pens or cards with capitalised words; Bibles for **Bible talk**
- Music charts (AASA4.May_1) on a card for each person and pens for **Prayer activity**
- **Prayer of confession** (AASA4.May_2) to display

All downloads are freely available from www.scriptureunion.org.uk/lightdownloads.

Beginning the service

With: appropriate people to illustrate 'closeness'

Explain that this service is looking at the life of David as King of all Israel. Ask what the children can recall of his life. Comment on how David had an energetic and close relationship with God and that there are at least three ways to understand 'closeness' as now demonstrated.

1 Ask several children to get as close as possible on a small rug or piece of newspaper. Ideally some of them will fall off so they have to get really close! This is one sort of physical closeness.
2 Ask two family members who look alike to come to the front and comment on their close likeness.
3 Ask two friends or family members who are close in their relationship to come forward and question them about the nature of their closeness and how they sustain it.

Bible reading

During a slow reading of Psalm 63, show images of a desert (verse 1), someone singing (verses 2–5), a bed (verse 6), an eagle or large bird (verse 7), one large hand holding a smaller one (verse 8) and a crown (verses 9–11). Alternatively, these could be mimed.

Bible retelling

This retelling of 2 Samuel 15–18 will remind people of the story of David in exile. It could include a mime.

Now Absalom was a handsome man – from the top of his head to the sole of his foot. A bit of an Adonis, if you like. He was one of King David's sons. David really loved him.

Absalom had ambitions. One day he wanted to be king – like his father. He couldn't wait for his father to die. In fact, he started to plan how he could take the throne now. He got himself a smart vehicle and a few supporters to 'big him up' – quite the royal prince. Each day, straight after breakfast, he would be waiting at the city gate to intercept people who wanted to see the king.

'Oh,' he would say, 'my father is too busy to see you! Look, anyone can see that your business here needs to be dealt with straightaway. Now

if I were in charge I'd see you immediately and grant you justice!' Then he would reach out his arms and give them a great big hug! The Bible tells us that he stole the hearts of the people.

It wasn't too long before Absalom set up a deal with his father's trusted adviser, Ahithophel, and declared himself king. When David heard of this, he knew he'd better get out of Jerusalem quick or he and his family and advisers would all be killed. He wept loudly as he left the city and the people who saw him pass by wept too. He climbed up the Mount of Olives where he met his friend Hushai who agreed to go to Jerusalem to spy on Absalom's activities.

David was deeply shocked and sad – no longer king, afraid for his life, hungry and thirsty and betrayed by his son. And so David waited in the desert. While there he wrote a song, 'Your love means more than life to me, God. I'm gonna stay really close to you.'

Back in Jerusalem, everybody trusted Ahithophel's advice. (After all, he had been David's most trusted adviser and he still gave the best advice out, but these days to 'King' Absalom, not 'King' David!) Ahithophel told Absalom to send his best men to assassinate the king. Minimum bloodshed. Good result.

But Absalom wasn't convinced. This strategy didn't sound grand enough. 'Let's see what Hushai has to say,' he said. Now Hushai was David's spy. He may have given good advice to David but he now had the task of giving bad advice to Absalom.

'Well', Hushai said, in a 'strokey-beardy' sort of way, 'Ahithophel's advice is not good. What if they finally fail and are caught? Nah. Better if you just get a great big army and attack David. Much the best thing!'

Absalom liked this advice better than what Ahithophel had recommended. So the two big armies met and guess who won? Yes. David's army. Hurrah! When he returned to Jerusalem he was very merciful to those who had treated him badly. He would have been kind to Absalom too but…what do you think happened to Absalom? He got his head caught in a tree as he was riding along and David's general, Joab, finished him off before David found out! But this made David very, very sad.

103

Bible talk

With: a flip chart or cards with the capitalised words below on them, to display; marker pen; Bibles; musicians

Explain that music was a big part of King David's life. The songs that you might sing later emphasise that the things that happened in David's life fed his communication with God.

David wrote many psalms; possibly as many as 78 are recorded in the Book of Psalms. Probably the most well known is Psalm 23. Refer back to Service 5. Ask if anyone can explain why David described God as his shepherd. They might mention David's earlier life as a shepherd near Bethlehem. Draw out good reasons why sheep would be safer when kept close to the shepherd. Explain that we will be kept safe when we stay close to God, our shepherd. Sing a verse of 'The Lord's my Shepherd' here. Write or display SHEPHERD on your flip chart.

What other words are there to describe David? After a few comments, write or show MUSICIAN on the flip chart. If possible play some harp music. David played the harp for King Saul, his predecessor, and he wrote songs and psalms.

Read the following verses, giving them their context. After each verse, ask what word or phrase you could write or display to describe his many roles.

2 Samuel 8:1,6b: Write or display WARRIOR or MILITARY LEADER. You could sing 'Our God is an awesome God' or 'Be bold, be strong'.

2 Samuel 9:1,13: Write or display KIND PROTECTOR. You could now sing 'Blessed be the name of the Lord…The name of the Lord is a strong tower'.

Psalm 51:1,2,10: Briefly tell the story of David and Bathsheba. People might then suggest 'Murderer' or 'Adulterer' but in the light of this psalm you would want to write SORRY FOR HIS SINS. You could now sing 'Purify my heart' or something similar.

2 Samuel 15:13–15: Recall the **Bible retelling**. Write or display REFUGEE or FUGITIVE. David had known what it was like to be chased by King Saul and to live as an outlaw. But now he was king. How dreadful for a king to be treated like this! So often his experiences had led him to call upon God and see how what he was facing helped him come close to God. This happened now.

Refer to Psalm 63 and, if possible, ask people to look it up in their Bibles.

Close in communicating with God

David remembered the times when God had seemed very close to him (verses 2–5) and he longed to be that close to God again, to be able to communicate like close friends and family do. God wants us all to be in such close contact with him. This is not just for King David.

Feeling God's closeness

David also wanted to feel God's closeness, to know he was protected, and cared for. He used active words in the psalm – ask what these words are – thirsting, seeing, singing, eating, excited, resting, held. We cannot see God but we can know that he is close and present all the time. This is as true for us as it was for King David.

Behaving in a way that is close to God

And when David returned to Jerusalem he behaved in a way that was like God – a family likeness. He showed mercy. Refer to the mercy he showed to Shimei in 2 Samuel 19:19–23. The more time we spend with God, the more we will bear the family likeness, a different sort of closeness. James refers to this in 4:7–10. Being close to God means that we will want to behave in a way that is like God and acceptable to him.

Three sorts of closeness – communicating closely with God, knowing God is close with us all the time, behaving in a way that is closely like God. Follow this with the **Prayer activity**.

Prayer activity

With: a copy of the card AASA4.May_1, for each person; pens

As music was important to David, so this activity is based around the music theme. Give out the cards and pens, then explain (for those who don't know) that the quaver is a short note (worth half a beat), while the minim is a longer one (worth two beats). The treble clef is for young and mainly women's voices while the bass clef is for men.

In this activity people will only complete one line, either treble or bass depending upon which applies to them.

In the Quaver box, everyone writes or draws a place or situation where they want to know God is close to them.

In the Minim box they write or draw a symbol of a longer conversation they want to have with God about how they want to be closer to God in the way that they behave. You will need to give a few suggestions or personal examples.

Play appropriate music to allow everyone to talk with God on their own.

Prayer of confession

With: the prayer (AASA4.May_2) on display for everyone to join in the emboldened words

This is a prayer that acknowledges that we often forget to trust in God's closeness.

David wrote: I think about you before I go to sleep.
Lord God, we have often forgotten to think about you at the beginning or close of the day. (*Pause*)
Please forgive us and help us to remember that you are close with us all the time.

David wrote: I stay close to you, and your powerful arm supports me.
Lord God, we have often relied on doing something in our own strength and have not allowed you to strengthen us. Lord, you are our refuge. (*Pause*)
Please forgive us and help us to remember that you are close by all the time to strengthen us.

David wrote: You have helped me and I sing…in the shadow of your wings.
Please help me when I am afraid to remember that you protect us all the time.

May we trust in you!
Amen

Ending the service

Ask people to stand with at least two other people, as close as they find comfortable. Then pray the following:

This week, go in the strength of the God of all comfort:
To places where you need never be alone,
God is close by you.
To people who may not want to communicate with you,
God is always close by to listen.
To situations where it is hard to be like Christ,
God is making you like himself.
Amen

Helpful extras

Music and song ideas

'Peace to you' *SOF* 460
'Purify my heart' *SOF* 475
'To be in your presence' *SOF* 1067
'As the deer pants' *SOF* 27
'My lips shall praise you' *SOF* 937
'The Lord's my shepherd' traditional *SOF* 537 or Stuart Townend *SOF* 1030
'What a friend we have in Jesus' *SOF* 593
'Our God is an awesome God' *ts* 418
'Be bold, be strong' *SOF* 37
'Leave all your worries' BSBS
'Come near' *BSBS2*

Harp music to use in the **Bible talk** – a live harpist, downloads from the Internet or a keyboard played on 'harp'.

Notes and comments

There is a lot of suggested music to highlight its importance in King David's life. Give your musicians plenty of preparation time.

For the **Bible reading**, an Internet search should find suitable images to display.
The **Prayer of confession** could be used as part of a service of Holy Communion.
Prayers of intercession could include prayer for those who are close by and those who are far away, both of whom can know God's closeness! You could particularly pray for those who are seeking to be like Jesus (behaving in a way that is close to him) in a challenging situation.

Pentecost

June

Light series: The gift of God's Spirit
Light readings: Acts 1:1−11; 2:1−13, 43−47

Aim: to celebrate the coming of the Holy Spirit
to see what the Spirit makes possible

Readings: Ezekiel 37:1−14; Acts 2:1−21

Getting started

Ezekiel prophesied from 593−573 BC. He lived in Babylon with others who had been taken into exile from Jerusalem. Jerusalem and the temple had been destroyed. With it, the exiles' hope was destroyed because the temple expressed God's presence with his people. They felt like dry bones with no hope for the future.

The Lord tells Ezekiel to prophesy to the bones. The bones were lying around, all higgledy-piggledy. Imagine Ezekiel's surprise when he hears a rattling noise and realises that the bones are coming together as bodies, but they were still lying lifeless. Ezekiel prophesies again, addressing the Holy Spirit. The word used throughout this passage is the Hebrew word 'ruach' which refers to the Spirit, breath and the wind. Now the bodies come to life, so many as to form a vast army. Seeing the bones become living bodies, the people begin to hope again that the Lord is still with them and that one day, he will take them home to Jerusalem.

All this is a picture of what happened on the first day of Pentecost. We say to the Lord that we don't want to be like dry bones. We want to be like the disciples: full of the Spirit, new life and power to share God's love with others. May your all-age service be filled with life this Pentecost!

You will need:

- (optional) six children in black with a white bone outline stuck to them, for the **Bible reading**
- a large outline drawing of a human skeleton, with all the major bones separated (see http:/www. lessontutor.com/jm_skeleton.html); flip chart; Blu-tack for the **Bible talk**
- enough balloons for every 2−3 people; wool, string or gift ribbon to hang up the balloons; jumbo marker pens with very thick tips (enough for every 2−3 people) for **Prayer activity**
- Prayer (AASA4.June_1) to display for **Ending the service**

All downloads are freely available from www.scriptureunion.org.uk/lightdownloads.

Beginning the service

Ask, 'What is the most essential thing we need in order to live?' (You're looking for the answer, 'oxygen'. You'll probably get other answers which will be correct which you can affirm, but keep asking until someone says 'oxygen' or 'breath'). Introduce the theme by saying that, as Christians, we need the Holy Spirit to live as God wants us to, just as much as we need oxygen. Today is Pentecost, when we celebrate the gift of the Holy Spirit to the followers of Jesus. We'll be thinking about how the Holy Spirit helps us.

Use this opening response, with everyone joining in the emboldened words:

God says, 'I will pour out my Spirit on everyone.'
Come, Holy Spirit!
Pour out your power on us.
Come, Holy Spirit!

Bible reading

Ezekiel 37:1–14 is very visual. Use the CEV to read it. You could do so with different people reading the parts of the narrator, Ezekiel and the Lord.

More dramatic would be to have six children dressed in black with one of six large bones stuck to them – two arms, two legs, a spine and a skull. At the start they lie down in a pile at the front or down the aisle. As verse 7 is read they clack together to become a body but they then stand still (or lie down), lifeless. As verse 10 is read they begin to dance around, still all joined together. This will be a challenge and will look odd but its meaning will be obvious and amusing. They freeze during the reading of verses 11–14 and then dance back to their seats. A glockenspiel could be played early on to give the effect of bones or the 'Fossils' from Saint Saens' *Carnival of the animals.*

Acts 2:1–21 also lends itself to a narrative reading with a narrator, a crowd and Peter. Sound effects could be introduced in the early part or swirling ribbons to give the effect of wind and fire.

Bible talk

With: a large outline drawing of a human skeleton, with all the major bones separated (for a good skeleton drawing see http://www. lessontutor.com/jm_skeleton.html); a flip chart stand; Blu-tack

The skeleton would work best if reproduced on black sugar paper using white poster paint. It needs to be big enough for everyone all over the building to see it. Cut out the skeleton into separate bones. Don't worry about having individual bones of the hands and feet, but the whole hand needs to be separate from the two arm bones, and the whole foot separate from the two leg bones.

Before the service, hide all the separate parts of the skeleton around the room. Count how many pieces you have before hiding them, so you can tell whether you've got them all once younger children have finished the bone hunt.

Begin by asking the younger children (those under 7) to hunt for bones. Tell them to bring any they find to the front. Encourage everyone else to call out where they can see bones. Once you have all the bones, ask people to help you put the skeleton together, sticking it on the flip chart. Working downwards would be the best way. Ask what you need to start with. Involve older children by asking for several to search through your pile of bones and hand you each bone as you ask for it. (You may want to 'ham it up', by playing thick about which bone you need next and deliberately putting them in the wrong place, so people can call out to tell you the correct way of doing it.)

Explain Ezekiel's situation, living in exile, with others from Jerusalem. The city was taken by enemies as God's punishment for the people ignoring God. Everyone felt that God had deserted them. They felt hopeless, like dry bones. Ezekiel's picture of bones getting back together again, with life breathed into them, was a picture of God breathing life into his people. It was his promise that, one day, he would rescue them and take them home to Jerusalem. It was something that only he could do by his Holy Spirit.

Left to our own devices, we are like dry bones: lifeless and powerless because we ignore God. But when we say sorry to God for ignoring him, he forgives us and breathes his Holy Spirit into us.

Peter's speech on the very first day of Pentecost (Acts 2:1–21) reminds us that because Jesus died for us, we can all have God's Holy Spirit living in us. Remind everyone of the story of that day and, if appropriate, sing the song for younger children that tells the story – see **Music and song ideas**. We need him to help us to live as

God wants us to, just as we need oxygen for our bodies to live. But just as Ezekiel needed to ask the Spirit to breathe into the bodies to make them come to life, so we need to ask the Spirit to breathe into us to help us to live as God wants us to.

Prayer activity

With: enough balloons for every 2–3 people; some wool, string or gift ribbon in order to hang the balloons up; jumbo marker pens with very thick tips (enough for every 2–3 people)

Hold up a deflated balloon. Ask everyone to try to write on a deflated balloon (which is a challenge!). Ask what you need to do to the balloon to make it possible to write on it. (Answer: blow it up.) Blow the balloon up, tying a knot to keep it inflated. Make the point that Ezekiel's bodies without God's breath were useless. When we pray, we need the breath of the Holy Spirit to help us. Now the balloon is blown up, it is possible to write on it. Ask for suggestions for prayer topics, based on the subject of our need of the Holy Spirit to fill us so that we can live as God's people.

In pairs or family groups, ask people to blow up their balloons, tying a knot, then a length of wool, to the neck. Ask an adult in each small group to write carefully on the balloon a short prayer based on the subjects discussed.

When everyone has finished their own prayer, ask people (children, where possible) to bat their balloon across the building to someone else. When people have a new balloon, ask them to pray the prayer on this new balloon. Repeat this two or three times, according to the time available and people's responsiveness. When you have finished, ask a couple of adults to gather the balloons together and bunch them together so they can be suspended around the building. People can see the prayers they've prayed.

Prayer of confession

The congregation joins in the emboldened refrain.

When we ignore you and go our own way,
Lord, have mercy: **Lord, have mercy.**

When we forget your presence with us, and become like dry bones,
Christ, have mercy. **Christ, have mercy.**

When we do things in our own strength and not yours,
Lord, have mercy. **Lord, have mercy.**

Father forgive us through the death of Jesus, your Son,
and strengthen us to live in the power of your Holy Spirit
today and every day.
Amen.

Ending the service

Remind everyone that Ezekiel's bones became bodies but didn't live until they were filled with the Holy Spirit. As Christians, we need to be constantly filled with the Holy Spirit. The closing prayer helps us to ask God to fill us with his Holy Spirit, so that we can live as he wants us to. Ask everyone to join in with the closing prayer (AASA4.June_1).

Heavenly Father, thank you for the gift of your Holy Spirit.
Fill us with your breath and power every day,
so that everyone may see through us that Jesus Christ is the Saviour of the world.
Amen.

If appropriate, give six balloons (not inflated) to each family group for them to create another Holy Spirit prayer for each day of next week. They are asking God to give them new life as individuals and as a family to live as God wants them to. You could also give a balloon to those who are sad or feeling hopeless, as a reminder of the hope that God gave to his people in exile. This would need to be handled sensitively.

Helpful extras

Music and song ideas

General music to play might be Saint-Saens' 'Fossils' from *Carnival of the animals* (see **Bible reading**) or the song 'Dem Dry Bones'. These can both be downloaded from iTunes for less than £1 each.

'Breathe on me, breath of God' *SOF* 51
'Come down, O love divine' *SOF* 1202
'O Thou who camest from above' *SOF* 451
'Rejoice, rejoice, Christ is in you' *SOF* 480
'Send us the rain, Lord' *SOF* 997 (the third verse picks up on the Ezekiel passage)
'These are the days of Elijah' *SOF* 1047 (the second verse speaks of Ezekiel)
'Like a gentle breeze' *SOF* 343
'Holy Spirit, we welcome you' *SOF* 188
'Spirit of the Living God' *SOF* 510 and 511 (there are two forms of this song which are both suitable but only use one as they're very similar)

These songs words below (AASA4.June_2) should be displayed, to tell the story of the first day of Pentecost. It goes to the tune of 'Here we go round the mulberry bush'. Make up actions for each verse as you sing it together. If you prefer, change the last line of each verse to: 'He came at Pentecost'.

Jesus promised a helper would come,
Helper would come, helper would come.
Jesus promised a helper would come,
On Holy Spirit Day.

The sound of a wind came filling the room,
Filling the room, filling the room.
The sound of a wind came filling the room,
On Holy Spirit Day.

A special fire touched all their heads,
All their heads, all their heads.
A special fire touched all their heads,
On Holy Spirit Day.

They then ran out to talk of God's love,
Talk of God's love, talk of God's love.
They then ran out to talk of God's love,
On Holy Spirit Day.

The Holy Spirit has come to stay,
Come to stay, come to stay.
The Holy Spirit has come to stay,
On Holy Spirit Day.

Notes and comments

It would be appropriate in the **Prayers of intercession** to pray for situations which seem lifeless and without hope, asking God by his Spirit to make a difference and bring life. This could be a war-torn zone in the world, or a long-standing dilemma facing the church or an individual. People could be given a bone-shaped card on which is written a prayer request. One request could be written on a set of six bone-shaped cards (two arms, two legs, a spine and a skull, as in the **Bible reading**). Everyone finds the five other bones with the same request to make a set and then in a group they make this prayer request. The bones fitted together create a body which then needs life to be breathed into it.

This outline has been adapted from *Light for the Lectionary April–June 2009*.

Peter, this is your life!

July

Light series: Living with Jesus
Light readings: Mark 1:16−20; 8:27−30; 9:2−13; 14:27−31,66−72; John 21:15−19

Aims: to review Peter's life up to when he met Jesus after the resurrection
to identify what it means for us to live with Jesus

Readings: Mark 1:16−20; John 21:15−19; Joel 2:12,13

Getting started

The readings from this *Light* series focus on five episodes from the period of Peter's life that he spent with Jesus. Each occasion presents a different characteristic of Peter, an ordinary man who experienced extraordinary things because he lived with Jesus. In this service, we will focus on Peter and how we are like or unlike him, and also see what it means to live with Jesus.

Living with Jesus is both wonderful and difficult. It is not easy for us, just as it was not easy for those who shared Jesus' earthly life. There are ups and downs in our perceptions and experiences of Jesus, because we are inconstant human beings. Sometimes we have moments of illumination − but sometimes we fail to follow him, in small ways or, sometimes, spectacularly.

Yet Jesus entrusted the Church to Peter, however flawed and human he was. Jesus forgave him, reinstated him, restored him and empowered him. He does all those things for us, too, so no matter how feeble we feel or how many mistakes we make, our connection with Jesus is always renewable and the invitation to live with him is a permanent one.

You will need

- PETER written vertically on two sheets of a flip chart; pen
- if learning the Learn and remember verse, the CD version − see **Music and song ideas**
- script for interview with Peter and an interviewee; optional big, red 'This is your life' book for the **Bible talk**
- a timeline for everyone (AASA4.July_1); pens and pencils for the **Prayer activity**

All downloads are freely available from www.scriptureunion.org.uk/lightdownloads.

Beginning the service

Explain that this service is going to be focused around the life of Peter, whom the children will have encountered in their groups. Show the five letters that spell his name and ask for words or phrases beginning with these four letters that describe Peter. These might include: pushy, puts his foot in it, practical, extrovert, energetic, enthusiastic, ebullient, terrified, talented, reckless, rushed, rough, rude.

Then explain that you have all come to worship God. What words or phrases can you think of that describe God, using these same four letters? These might include: powerful, present, people-loving, everywhere, energetic, everlasting, tower of strength, trustworthy, truthful, right, righteous, ruler, reigning.

Include as many of these words as you can in an introductory prayer, followed by songs of worship and praise to God.

Bible reading

During the **Bible talk**, several passages from Mark and John will be read. Make sure that the person who reads them has practised and reads with clarity and warmth.

The Learn and remember verse for this series is Joel 2:13b which in the GNB reads: 'Come back to the Lord your God. He is kind and full of mercy; he is patient and keeps his promise; he is always ready to forgive and not punish.' This is available in a song version as 'Come back' *Bitesize Bible Songs* CD (SU).

Learn the verse (and the song if appropriate) commenting that the prophet Joel probably delivered this message to the people of God when they were living in exile. (Refer to Service outline 11, which focused on Ezekiel's prophetic ministry.) God called the people back to himself and offered them hope. Peter made all kinds of mistakes but Jesus restored him and gave him hope. If the children already know the song, invite them to lead the singing.

Bible talk

With: an actor playing Peter; someone who has agreed to answer the same questions as Peter's about their own life; a prepared person to read the Bible; optional big, red 'This is your life' book

First, carry out an interview with the adult who will give their personal testimony, using the 'This is your life' book if appropriate.

- Why did you think it was worth following Jesus? (Answer focuses on what the person found interesting about Jesus. They should not talk about the influence of other people.)
- But there's more to Jesus than that, isn't there? Was there one time when you realised who he really was or was it a more gradual process? (Answer should either focus on a spiritual revelation when 'the penny dropped' or acknowledge that realising who Jesus is can often happen over a period of time. Whatever response you get, assure everyone that we all come to Jesus in our unique way. We are all different.)
- Would you say you were a good friend to Jesus? (Answer in terms of 'could do better', mentioning failings, but acknowledging that he goes on loving us and being our friend.)
- Have you ever felt stunned by an experience of living with Jesus? (Answer should focus on an unusual event which was awe-inspiring, perhaps unnerving.)

Then ask these same questions of the actor playing Peter, using the 'This is your life' book.

- Why did you think it was worth following Jesus? (Peter tells the story from John 1:35−42 and then says, 'Listen to how my friend John Mark writes about it. He kept a close account of what Jesus said and did. It's in his gospel.' Read out Mark 1:16−18.)
- But there's more to Jesus than that, isn't there? Was there a time when you realised who Jesus really was? (Peter tells how he had several experiences when things became clearer but then tells in more detail the story of the Transfiguration from Mark 9:2−13. Peter concludes by referring to the statement he made about Jesus just before this happened. Peter says, 'Listen to how my friend John Mark writes about it. It's in his gospel.' Read Mark 8:27−30.)
- Would you say you were a good friend to Jesus? (Peter talks about being one of the closest three disciples to Jesus, witnessing the Transfiguration. But he deserted Jesus at the arrest in the garden. Peter begins to tell the story of his denial of Jesus, which was when he realised what a poor friend he was – but says, 'Listen to how my friend John Mark writes about it. It's in his gospel.' Read Mark 14:66−72.)
- Have you ever felt stunned by an experience of living with Jesus? (Peter tells the story of

his meeting on the beach with Jesus after the resurrection from John 21:1–14. After this, Peter knew he was forgiven and had a role to play in spreading the good news of Jesus. Read John 21:13–17.)

Conclude by saying that Peter was to learn what it meant to live for Jesus. Open the 'This is your life' book and ask rhetorically what people would want to put in this book about their own life with Jesus. You will need to explain the 'This is your life' concept which may not be known by younger people! (If appropriate, you could ask people to break into groups to talk about this.) Comment that we all let Jesus down, just as Peter did. But just like him, we can also be forgiven, making a fresh start. This is what life with Jesus means.

Sing or say the Learn and remember verse again.

Prayer activity

With: a simple timeline for everyone (AASA4. July_1); pens and pencils

This should follow on directly from the **Bible talk**. Give everyone a timeline which is marked as follows, working left to right:
Date of birth; a time when I knew Jesus loved me; a time when I knew Jesus had forgiven me; a time when I said or did something to help others hear about Jesus.
Emphasise that we can all come to Jesus in different ways and some people may not be sure yet whether they know his love and forgiveness.

Ask everyone to complete the timeline for themselves, writing or drawing symbols of the significant times. You could show how it works by completing your own timeline for everyone to see or by doing one for the person who was interviewed. Conclude by giving time for everyone to talk with Jesus, thanking him that he is our friend and never gives up on us.

Alternatively, you could make mini red books labelled 'This is your life' and invite people to write something in their book and then talk with God about what they have written. They could take this home or do this as an **Ending the service** activity.

Prayer of confession

Peter let Jesus down. And he was deeply sorry about this. He needed to be forgiven so he could go on living with Jesus.

Jesus Christ, there are times this week when we have said things which a friend of yours should not say. (*Pause*)
Please forgive us.
Jesus Christ, there are times this week when we have done things which a friend of yours should not do. (*Pause*)
Please forgive us.
Jesus Christ, there are times when we have pretended that we are not your friend, when we have not loved you and when we have not enjoyed your company. (*Pause*)
Please forgive us.
Jesus forgave Peter and gave him an important task to do. He promises to forgive all those who admit they have done wrong and want to put things right. His Spirit enables us to live for Jesus.

Day by day, O Lord, three things I pray:
to see thee more clearly;
to love thee more dearly;
to follow thee more nearly, day by day.
Amen

A prayer of Richard of Chichester (1197–1253)

Prayers of intercession

It would be appropriate to pray for any activities that are occurring now or in the near future that are seeking to introduce people to Jesus that they might become his friend. This might include a holiday club, Christian holiday activity or an Alpha-type course. It is an opportunity to pass on information and encourage prayer by the whole church.
It might be appropriate to prepare a bookmark (or mini red book) to give to everyone before the prayer time for them to take home.

Ending the service

With: PETER written vertically on a flip chart – see **Beginning the service**; pen

So, how can we live with Jesus, this week? Ask for words or phrases that begin with the letters of Peter's name. This might include: pray, persevere, patient, energetic, explain about Jesus, exceptionally helpful, expectant of God, truthful, trusting, talking to lonely people, reassuring, reading the Bible, reflecting on Jesus.

Helpful extras

Music and song ideas

'All that I am, all that I do' *SOF* 647
'O Jesus, I have promised' *SOF* 418
'Jesus put this song into our hearts' *SOF* 299
'Purify my heart' *SOF* 475
'Lord of all hopefulness' *SOF* 902
'Dear Lord and Father of mankind' *SOF* 79
'I reach up high' *SOF* 1358
Come back' *BSBS* – the Learn and remember
verse for Joel 2:13b
'God is an awesome God' *LFE*
'When you make a mistake' *RU*

Notes and comments

To help you explain what it means to be a
follower of Jesus, get hold of a copy of *Top
Tips on Helping a child respond to Jesus*, which
identifies four ways in which people responded
to Jesus in the New Testament. There were
other ways, but the point is that we are all
individuals and come to Jesus in the way that
best suits us and our backgrounds. This book is
actually relevant for adults and young people.

In this service there is a challenge to everyone
to consider how they have responded to Jesus,
both now and in the past. Younger children may
not be able to articulate it clearly (but that is
true for many adults too). Try to present a clear
and sensitive challenge to everyone to go on
living with Jesus from this point on. You will want
to have some literature to pass on to anyone
who wants to know more. *Jesus=friendship
forever, Me+Jesus* and *Friends with Jesus* are three
Scripture Union booklets you would want to
use with under 12s.

There are many more resources, based on
episodes from Peter's life, available from SU,
including the Scripture Union holiday club
programmes, *Seaside Rock* and *Rocky's Plaice*
with the accompanying DVDs, *Take Away* (an
eyelevel midweek club programme) and the
children's book, *Peter puts his foot in it.*

**Top tips on helping a
child respond to Jesus**

978 1 84427 387 4

Booklets to use with children who want to
know what it means to respond to Jesus

Friends with Jesus
978 1 84427 141 2
(for 5–7s)

Me and Jesus
978 1 84427 142 9
(for 8–9s)

**Jesus=friendship
forever**
978 1 84427 143 6
(for 10–12s)

Holiday club and midweek club material

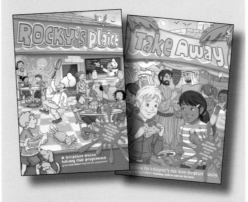

Rocky's Plaice
978 1 84427 390 4

Take Away
978 1 84427 502 1

For more details go to
www.scriptureunion.org.uk/shop

The world's best-seller

August

Light series: Adventures with God
Light readings for the month: Acts 8:26–40; 9:32–43; 10:1–48; 12:1–19

Aim: to encourage people to value and use the Bible which is inspired by God

Readings: Psalm 119:97–105,127; 2 Timothy 3:16

Getting started

August sees a change to routines and rhythms as many people are refreshed at home or away. This service outline seeks to refresh people's commitment and passion to the Bible, the world's best-seller. It draws together the *Light* theme on the early church, in particular Acts 8: 26–40 which describes Philip's encounter with the Ethiopian who was struggling to understand the Scriptures he was reading. This struggle is an experience common to many of us. Make sure that Bibles are available and that throughout the service the Bible has a high and enthusiastic profile. Passion for the Bible is more often caught than taught.

Psalm 119 is so long, but at its very heart is an excitement about God's Word, with a desire for it to shape life. Verses 97–105 and 127 reflect this passion. Centuries later, Paul exhorts the young pastor Timothy to look to the God-given Scripture that he has grown up with, a vital source of guidance and wisdom. Although he was primarily referring to the Pentateuch, Christians believe this principle should be applied to the whole of the Bible.

The outline recognises that a service during the summer months needs to be self-standing.

You will need

- honey sandwiches; labelled honey jars, torches and bags of pretend gold coins (see **Beginning the service** for the wording on the labels)
- volunteers for the **Bible reading**
- a rucksack containing four or five popular books; a Bible; the words of 2 Timothy 3:16 displayed on a screen; a whistle, for **the Bible talk**
- ten statements about the Bible and a copy of the Prayer (AASA4.Aug_1) for the **Prayer activity**
- Pictures of honey, gold and torches (AASA4.Aug_2) for **Ending the service**
- two simple Lego models for the **Game**

All free downloads are available from www.scriptureunion.org.uk/lightdownloads.

Beginning the service

With: honey sandwiches; jars of honey labelled: 'Your teachings are sweeter than honey. Psalm 119:103'; torches labelled: 'Your word is a lamp that gives light wherever I walk. Psalm 119:105'; bags of pretend gold coins labelled: 'Your laws mean more to me than the finest gold. Psalm 119:127'.

Place the honey, torches and gold around the church. Having multiples of each item allows more people to be involved in the activity.

Prior to the formal start, offer honey sandwiches to everyone. Once everyone has been welcomed, ask them to hunt for clues to the theme of the service. The clues all have a label with a Bible verse.

Arrange the three groups of items in three piles – honey, torches and bags of gold. Each group should read out their Bible verse. When the honey verse is read, make reference to the honey sandwiches and emphasise how sweet they were.

Ask the congregation to guess what the focus of the service could be – expect the answer 'the Bible'. Explain that the writer of Psalm 119 was passionate about God's Word, and that the aim of the service is to encourage everyone to see how valuable and useful the Bible is. Leave the items at the front to use during the **Bible talk**.

Bible reading

Psalm 119 enthuses about God's Word and verses 97 to 105 and verse 127 capture this passion. For a sense of vitality and poignancy, the verses could be read by three children or young people, who should practise together – see below.

A,B,C: I deeply love your Law! I think about it all day.

A: Your laws never leave my mind, and they make me much wiser than my enemies.

B: Thinking about your teachings gives me better understanding than my teachers,

C: And obeying your laws makes me wiser than those who have lived a long time.

A: I obey your word instead of following a way that leads to trouble.

B: You have been my teacher, and I won't reject your instructions.

C: Your teachings are sweeter than honey.

A: They give me understanding and make me hate all lies.

B: Your word is a lamp that gives light wherever I walk.

C: Your laws mean more to me than the finest gold.
Psalm 119: 97–105, 127 (CEV)

---

2 Timothy 3:16 communicates the authority and value of God's Word. Teach four simple actions to aid memory and to facilitate the involvement of young children – see below. You may prefer to use a translation such as the TNIV which, although less accessible to children, does use the word 'God-breathed'.

Everything (*draw a large circle with two hands*) in the Scriptures is God's Word (*blow hard onto hands as they move forward to create an open book shape*). All of it is useful (*make a capital U with thumbs and forefingers*) for teaching and helping people and for correcting them and showing them how to live (*tap finger on side of head*). 2 Timothy 3:16 (CEV).

Ask everyone to listen out for a signal (such as a blown whistle) throughout the service. Then display the Bible verse and encourage everyone to join in with the words and actions. This is the Learn and remember verse for the *Light* series, also available in a song format called 'Everything' *Bitesize Bible Songs* CD (SU).

Bible talk

With: a rucksack containing four or five popular books; a Bible; the words of 2 Timothy 3:16 displayed on a screen; a whistle; items from **Beginning the service**

This talk divides into two: to communicate that the Bible is special, and that it is useful.

The Bible is special
Show the rucksack and talk about how a holiday gives you an opportunity for holiday reading. Take the books out of the bag, asking which anyone would want to take on their holiday. Make sure the books appeal to a wide range of

interests and ages.

Take a Bible out of the rucksack and remind people that this is the world's best-seller, which has sold between 2.5 and 6 billion copies worldwide, according to Wikipedia. Make comparisons with the holiday books above and say that the Bible contains adventures, poems, songs, advice, letters and biographies. But it is not this that makes the Bible special.

Give the signal (*blown whistle*) for everyone to say 2 Timothy 3:16 whilst doing the actions.

Explain that the Bible is special because it is inspired by God. In his letter, Paul tells Timothy that Scripture is God-breathed. Refer to the first part of 2 Timothy 3:16: 'All Scripture is God-breathed.' (Paul uses the Greek word 'breathed' about the Bible, to mean it is inspired by God.) God helped human beings to write down what he wanted people to know about himself. Clarify that although Paul was referring to the Old Testament Scriptures when he wrote to Timothy, Christians believe this can be applied to the whole of the Bible.

God wants us to know what he is like, to see how we should live and, most importantly, to understand the difference Jesus has made. This is mysterious, puzzling and amazing. It makes the Bible different from any other book, and it's why the Bible is called 'God's Word'.

Refer to Psalm 119:103 and 127 which say that God's Word is sweeter than honey and more precious than gold because it's God message. Ask for a volunteer to collect a jar of honey and a bag of gold and put them in your rucksack. Give the signal for 2 Timothy 3:16 to be said again (*blown whistle*).

Ask people to consider whether they think the Bible is something special. Then take a break to sing a song such as 'Have you got an appetite?' (see **Music and song ideas**). This is a good point to play the **Game**.

The Bible is useful
Give the signal for everyone to say 2 Timothy 3:16 (*blown whistle*). Paul tells Timothy that Scripture is special, but it is also useful. Refer to the second half of the verse '…for teaching and helping people and for correcting and showing them how to live.'

Paul wanted Timothy to use God's Word to guide him and his friends on how they should

live. Refer to the **Game**, if it was played. The picture and the instructions showed the contestant the best way to build the model. As we read the Bible we sometimes see how we need to change what we think or what we do.

Ask a volunteer to collect a torch and put it in the rucksack. Psalm 119:105 says that God's Word is also useful like a torch, essential in the dark, especially on camping trips or when you are lost. Psalm 119 says it's good to think about and obey God's Word. The Bible can be hard to understand, and so we need to use our brain, talk to people and discuss it. Make reference to the meeting between the Ethiopian and Philip which is in the August *Light* series. Give examples of how members of the congregation can help each other understand the Bible. As well as understanding it, we should do what it says, most importantly by following Jesus.

Give the signal for 2 Timothy 3:16 to be said (*blown whistle*). Recap by showing everyone the honey, gold and torch, reminding them that the Bible is special and useful. Conclude by putting the Bible in the rucksack. It will be part of *your* holiday reading.

You could ask someone to give a brief testimony about how the Bible has really helped them.

Prayer activity
With: ten large statements placed around the church (see below); the prayer (AASA4.Aug_1) displayed on a screen or on the service sheet

This activity lets people pray through movement and words. The statements express a range of responses to the Bible: 'I think the Bible is confusing'; 'I like Bible stories'; 'I'd need help to understand the Bible'; 'The Bible is really interesting'; 'I find it hard to read the Bible'; 'I want a deeper understanding of the Bible'; 'I'd like to understand more of the Old Testament'; 'I'd like to understand more of the New Testament'; 'I like having the Bible read to me'; 'I've got lots of questions about the Bible'. Psalm 119:105 is the inspiration for the collective prayer.

Give the congregation five minutes to walk around, read the statements and discuss together which ones they agree with or not. Encourage adults to help children express their own opinions on the statements. On your prompting, ask everyone to stand close to one statement that they agree with. They should imagine they are saying this statement to God. The whole congregation then says this collective prayer. Repeat this movement twice, so that everyone has chosen three statements and prayed three times.

Father,
your Word is like a lamp.
It shines a light on the path showing me
how to live for you.
May I walk for you in the right way.
Amen

Prayers of intercession

With: people who share the Bible with others, for example missionaries or volunteers involved in holiday clubs or home group leaders

Briefly interview the representatives about how they try to open up people's eyes to the Bible. Also ask for specific prayer requests. Use this information to influence short prayers of thanks and petition. If a wide range of people are involved in activities such as holiday clubs, ask them to stand up so you can pray for them.

Ending the service

With: a pencil or pen; a picture of the torch, honey jar or bag of gold (AASA4.Aug_2) for each person present

Distribute a picture and pen to everyone. Ask them to draw a picture of the Bible in the middle of their picture, to be taken away as a reminder of the importance and use of the Bible. Give the signal to say 2 Timothy 3:16 together (*blown whistle*).

The hymn 'When we walk with the Lord' is suitably encouraging and challenging to conclude the service.

Helpful extras

Music and song ideas

'Thy word is a lamp to my feet' *SOF* 1066
'Have you got an appetite?' *ts* 145
'When we walk with the Lord' *SOF* 599
'We are marching in the light of God' *ts* 539
'Open my eyes that I might see' *MP* 544
'Everything' *BSBS* is the Learn and remember verse song for 2 Timothy 3:16.

Instrumental music can create a mood of

excitement during the **Game** and a sense of calm during the **Prayer activity**.

Game

With: two competitors; two simple Lego models unassembled

Hold a competition between two competitors to assemble a Lego model. One person should be given the bricks in a bag but have no picture or instructions. The second person should be given the bricks in a box with a picture and instructions. Give them two minutes to make their model. Encourage cheering and accompany the activity with lively background music. The person with the instructions and picture should win, so ensure this happens by asking the person without the instructions to go slow, if necessary.

It helps to know what something should be like and how it works best. The Bible shows us what God is like and the best way for us to live.

Notes and comments

If there is a baptism, give the family a child-friendly Bible such as *The Big Bible Storybook* (SU). Alternatively, the audio CD *Listen with the Bible* (SU) makes an excellent gift for under 8s and tells a wide range of Bible stories.

This service could be used to start a programme of activities to encourage people to get excited about reading and applying the Bible to their lives. After the service, display, or have for sale, various resources and suggestions for people to look at. Consider signing up for Scripture Union's Bible Enthusiasts scheme which provides access to a range of resources and look out for *Essential 100* on www.scriptureunion.org.uk

Miraculous God

September

Light series: Elijah the prophet
Light readings: 1 Kings 17; 18; 19:1–21; 21:1–19; 22:29–40

Aims: to meet Elijah, whom God used in powerful ways
to recognise how God comes to those who are in need

Readings: 1 Kings 17:17–24; John 2:1–11

Getting started

The *Light* series highlights a religious power struggle (1 Kings 17–19). On the one side there
is a fertility god (Baal) and on the other, the Lord God. Ahab and his foreign wife, Jezebel, are
representatives of Baal, and Elijah is the messenger of God. The Baals were thought to control the
weather, the cycle of agriculture, life and fertility, and the lightning and rain. Through Elijah, however,
God shows that he is the one who is in control. God controls the weather; he sends drought
(17:1–7) and rain (18:41–46). God controls the availability of food; he gives bread (17:8–16). God
controls life; he revives the widow's son (17:17–24). God controls lightning; he sends fire to burn up
the sacrifice (18:38). Here is a series of miracles or acts of power. God comes to those in human
need, as we can see with Elijah, the widow and her dead son. Similarly, Jesus miraculously came to the
rescue when the wine ran out at a wedding (John 2:1–10).

During September people start to think about harvest. Today's equivalent for Baal is Mother Nature.
Many assume that she will send the weather, provide the food and guarantee fertility. Like Elijah we
proclaim that the real power behind nature is God, the one who creates life and sustains natural
cycles.

You will need

• for the **Bible talk**: a marker pen; five large signs on poles made of card as follows: 'DO NOT
  ENTER!', 'DEAD SON!', 'BE SAD!', 'NO WINE!' and 'PANIC!' – allow space to add the words 'DO
  NOT' in front of 'BE SAD!' and 'PANIC!'
• a script for telling the story in John 2:1–10 (AASA4.Sept_1)
• a piece of paper in the shape of a water pot for everyone; pens for **Prayer activity**
• writing equipment for each group for the **Game**

All downloads are freely available from www.scriptureunion.org.uk/lightdownloads.

Beginning the service

With: a recording of, or the means to sing, 'Our God is an awesome God, He reigns from heaven above.'

Ask what it means to describe someone as 'awesome'. Who are the people anyone would describe as 'awesome'? Explain that the focus of the service is on our awesome God, his works of power and his miraculous deeds as he comes to those in need.

Then listen to or sing the words of 'Our God is an awesome God'. Vary the speed and volume as you sing it several times.

Bible reading

The reading from 1 Kings 17:17–24 can be read by a narrator (N), and two character voices – (the widow (W) and Elijah (E). The version below is adapted from the TNIV.

> **N:** Elijah was staying in a foreign town where he was looked after by a widow. The son of the woman who owned the house became ill. He grew worse and worse, and finally stopped breathing. In her anguish the woman turned on Elijah.
>
> **W to E:** (in accusing voice) What do you have against me, man of God? Was your real reason in coming here to remind me of my sin and kill my son?
>
> **E to W:** Give me your son.
>
> **N:** Elijah took the son from her arms, carried him to the upper room where he was staying, and laid him on his bed. Then Elijah cried out to the LORD.
>
> **E:** LORD my God, have you brought tragedy even on this widow I am staying with, by causing her son to die?
>
> **N:** Then Elijah stretched himself over the boy three times and cried to the LORD.
>
> **E:** O LORD my God, let this boy's life return to him!
>
> **N:** The LORD heard Elijah's cry, and the boy's life returned to him, and he lived. Elijah picked up the child and carried him down from the room into the house. He gave him to his mother.

> **E:** Look, your son is alive!
>
> **W to E:** Now I know that you are a man of God and that the word of the LORD from your mouth is the truth. *Pause*
>
> **W,E,N:** Now to the King eternal, immortal, invisible, the only God, be honour and glory for ever and ever. Amen.
>
> I Kings 17:17–24 (TNIV)

The story in John 2:1–10 is well known, so read it in a modern version such as *The Message*.

Bible retelling

1 Kings 17:17–24
(*told by a gossipy neighbour*)
Not a lot usually happens down our way but yesterday was different.

Recently there has been this foreign guy from Israel staying at my neighbours.' Foreign sounding name, as you'd expect…El-i-jah. That's it El-i-jah. A religious guy who prays to his God…

Now our neighbour is a poor widow. She has a son to look after. She's obviously not well off but has been providing B&B for this religious guy… the name again…El-i-jah… she's been feeding him as well as feeding herself and her son.

Well her son was taken ill and then he died. She was beside herself and rather unfairly took it out on this foreigner. She accused him of staying only to torment her and punish her for her wrongdoings. We all heard her raging. But, calm as you like, El-i-jah takes the dead boy, carries him up to his own guest room and cries out to his God. Seems to be asking this God why he's allowed the lad to die. Then he stretches himself over the boy's body – didn't seem bothered to be touching a dead person. And the boy came back to life…was revived…resuscitated…use what word you like.

What it all boils down to is that the lad was dead one minute…alive the next! That's a miracle in my book. His God has power. Mother and son were reunited. This foreigner, well as the lady says, this foreigner must be… a man of God.

The story when Jesus turned water into wine is well told in Episode 2 of *Wastewatchers* DVD (SU). The script of that episode (AASA4.Sept_1),

which could be read out loud, is available from
www.scriptureunion.org.uk/lightdownloads.

Bible talk

With: a marker pen; five large signs made of
card as follows: 'DO NOT ENTER!', 'DEAD
SON!', 'BE SAD!', 'NO WINE!' and 'PANIC!'
– allow space to add the words 'DO NOT' in
front of 'BE SAD!' and 'PANIC!' (Each sign can be
placed in a different area of the worship space
so that the idea of God being everywhere is
being acted out during the talk.)

Each sign is dealt with in turn.

DO NOT ENTER!
At the time of Elijah, people often thought God
was confined just to one place or territory.
But Elijah knew that God was more than that.
In today's story, God sent Elijah to a foreign
country, Phoenicia, and he sent him, as his
messenger, to a town called Zarephath near a
city called Sidon. Elijah went to this foreign land,
not with a timid spirit but trusting in God. He
was showing that there is no area where God
cannot go! God was breaking any boundary that
limited him. Break up the 'DO NOT ENTER!'
sign.

Elijah trusted in God and this gave him courage.
If appropriate, teach (or review) the Learn and
remember verse from 2 Timothy 1:7: 'For the
Spirit that God has given us does not make us
timid; instead, his Spirit fills us with power, love
and self-control.' To learn this as a song, see
Music and song ideas. Stress the idea of not
being timid and speak the second part boldly.

DEAD SON!
The woman had seen God provide them with
food in a miraculous way, but in her shock and
grief she accused Elijah of bringing tragedy to
her family. She panicked. Check that everyone
knows what Elijah did next and how Elijah
demonstrated God's power and compassion.
Break up the 'DEAD SON!' sign.

BE SAD!
The woman was deeply sad and distressed
when her son died. But she discovered that God
answered prayer and that Elijah was a prophet
of an all-powerful God – see verse 24. She did
not need to be sad. God, who gives life to all,
gave new life to her son. Instead of destroying
this sign (it is not true), change it to read 'DO
NOT BE SAD!'

NO WINE!
At the wedding Jesus went to, they ran out of
wine. It was a disaster for the man in charge of
the wedding festivities. It could have brought
shame on the family. But Jesus, who was God
and therefore had power, authority and also
compassion, did something to change everything.
Ask what he did. Then break up the sign.

PANIC!
Several people, including the servants and Jesus'
mother, were panicking that they had run out
of wine at the wedding. But because Jesus did
something to make a difference they no longer
needed to worry. Add 'DO NOT' or 'DON'T' to
the sign.

Boundaries, sadness and panic (or fear) can
prevent us from enjoying God's friendship. What
we are left with are two signs that say what we
must do if we trust in an awesome, powerful
God. We do not need to be sad and we do not
need to panic. There is no place where God
cannot be or go. So he is with us all the time.
There is no need that he cannot meet. Repeat
the Learn and remember verse from
2 Timothy 1:7.

Prayer activity

With: a piece of paper for everyone, in the
shape of a water pot; pens

God works through ordinary people who trust
him. Often it is through our actions that God
shows his power and compassion. It was through
Elijah that God showed his care for the woman.
God is active in ordinary situations too, such
as a wedding. How might God want to bless
someone else through each person present?

Comment that the water pot is empty. Ask
everyone to draw a line where the liquid would
be if the pot was full up. Then ask everyone to
write or draw something that they could do to
help someone in need (someone sad, afraid, sick
or alone in some way) this week so that their
life does not feel empty.

Then pray as follows:
Lord, we thank you that you are great and
powerful. Yet you choose us to share your love.
May we share your love with others.
May we share our homes, our hospitality, our
toys and our time.
May we give our time to help those in need and
in trouble in some way.
Use us, we pray, in Jesus' name. Amen.

Ending the service

Hundreds of years ago people used to look out west from Cornwall, France and Spain. All they could see were waves and the ocean. They thought there was nothing else beyond. Then in 1492 Columbus discovered America. Everything changed.

Some people look out on life and all they can see is things going wrong, emptiness, sorrow and pain. God acted in the life of the widow and everything changed. God acted to turn water into wine at the wedding and everything changed. Jesus came alive again and everything changed.

Close as you began, by singing 'Our God is an awesome God', only now we appreciate more fully just how awesome and powerful he is. Alternatively, you could sing 'God is an awesome God' from *Light for everyone* CD, which provides a list of the powerful things that Jesus did – see **Music and song ideas**.

Helpful extras

Music and song ideas

'Our God is an awesome God' *ts* 418
'God is an awesome God' *LFE*
'All my days' *SOF* 1158
'The Lord's my Shepherd' *SOF* 1030
'O Lord my God' *SOF* 425
'You are the King of Glory' SOF 627
'God's Spirit' *BSBS2*, the Learn and remember verse for 2 Timothy 1:17.

Game

With: paper and pen
Give paper and a pen to groups of two or three, challenging them to write or draw as many powerful things that they can think of in three minutes – anything at all that is powerful. Each group in turn then tells everyone what they have on their list. As each thing is mentioned, anyone else who has written it down crosses it off their list. Which group had the longest list?

Ask the children what they think is the most powerful.

Statement of faith

The song 'Our God is an awesome God' is a statement of faith that recurs throughout the service.

Notes and comments

The manner of the resuscitation by Elijah could be sensitive as Elijah stretched himself out on the boy three times. Remarkably, Elijah did not avoid contact with unclean death, as might be expected, but embraced death and through him God restored the dead back to life.

The words 'power and authority' may have negative connotations for some. Take the opportunity to present God, who holds ultimate authority, in a wholly positive light. Make sure that the prayer team is available to pray for those in need.

In the **Bible talk**, reference was made to God being everywhere and not territorially limited. In the light of this, pray for your mission partners who have certainly put this truth about God into practice by going to serve God elsewhere.

This is an adapted outline from *All-Age Lectionary Services Year A.*

Service 15

A festival to remember

Harvest a seasonal service, to use when appropriate for your church

Aims: to rejoice in God's provision at 'Harvest' and rely on God for his continued blessing and protection
to remember God's great acts of salvation in history

Readings: Leviticus 23:33–44

Getting started

This harvest service is shaped by the Feast of Shelters (*Sukkot* or Tabernacles) which emphasises both **rejoicing** in the (fruit) harvest and **remembering** the time the people spent in the desert after being set free from Egypt. The Feast of Shelters is an important festival for the Jewish community. More information on this festival (AASA4.Harvest_8) is available online. The celebrations involve the best fruit, waving the branches of various trees and building a temporary shelter as a reminder of the time the Israelites spent living in tents.

This harvest service should help everyone to celebrate all that God provides and to remember our dependence on God. Through building a shelter, the service includes an opportunity for people to identify themselves with the experience of God's people in the desert and to remember the times in our own lives where we have learned more of what it means to depend on God. A number of additional resources are available online.

In any special decoration of the church for harvest, bear in mind the 'fruit' element of the theme for the service. If you usually invite people to bring harvest gifts, encourage gifts with a fruit theme, including the 'fruit' of people's skills and work of many kinds.

You will need

- words of the acclamation (AASA4.Harvest_1) for **Beginning the service**
- optional script (and actors) or audio file (AASA4.Harvest_2); materials for making the shelter already built in advance for **Bible retelling**
- props and individuals prepared to share their relevant experience for the **Bible talk**
- a piece of damaged fruit for the **Prayer of confession**
- fruits from across the world for the **Game**
- small 'flags'; pencils; a tray of sand (part of the shelter) for **Prayers of intercession**
- bowls of fruit for **Ending the service**
- the following optional resources are available online: Bible readings and ideas for joining in the 'Hallel' (AASA4.Harvest_ 4); ideas for making streamers and providing prayers for younger children (AASA4.Harvest_5); ideas to make the most of your harvest festival (AASA4.Harvest_ 6); take home sheets for everyone that extend harvest into the rest of the week (AASA4.Harvest_ 7); Bible background (AASA4.Harvest_8)

All downloads are freely available from www.scriptureunion.org.uk/lightdownloads.

Beginning the service

Introduce the service as a harvest celebration with a difference. Every year, we celebrate the harvest of good things that God has given us. But our celebrations today will also help us think about the Festival of Shelters – the festival that God instructed his people to hold each year at the end of the fruit harvest. It is still celebrated by the Jewish community around the world. One of the instructions for the festival was for everyone to enjoy themselves. That is how this service will begin!

Divide the congregation into two parts, A and B. Say the words of this shout of acclamation (AASA4.Harvest_1). Saying it more than once will help participation by those who cannot read. (The same praise shout could be repeated before each of the songs in the service.)

All: Shout for joy to the Lord, all the earth.
A: Serve the Lord and be glad;
B: Come to him with joyful songs.
All: The Lord is good;
A: His love goes on for ever
B: His faithful love never fails.
(Adapted from Psalm 100:1,5)

Announce your first song and, if appropriate, invite people to bring forward their harvest gifts.

Bible reading

Introduce Leviticus 23:39–43 as the instructions for the Festival of Shelters. Ask the congregation to listen out for what the people were instructed to do, in addition to being happy.

Bible retelling

With: optional audio script or the script itself (AASA4.Harvest_2) *Building the Shelter* which, if read live, requires four performers

Ask if anyone has ever slept outside, perhaps on a camping holiday. Invite people to call out single words to describe what that was like.

Explain that the centre piece of the Festival of Shelters (called 'Sukkot' in Hebrew) is the construction of a simple temporary shelter. Jewish families construct such a shelter outside their homes which stays up for the whole week-long celebration of the Feast. In warmer climates families will live in the shelter for the whole week. By tradition, the roof of the shelter must have gaps so that the stars can be seen. Invite volunteers of all ages to build a shelter. Explain that they are like an Israelite household building their shelter for the festival together. The frame of a small family-sized tent or a gazebo is ideal for the framework. Blankets would be fine for the walls and use scatter cushions for the interior. Try to cover the roof with leafy branches such as willow and myrtle. Use string and clothes pegs to hang fruits and flowers around the shelter. The traditional harvest gifts can also be placed in and around the shelter. Place a small table inside with an (unlit) candle or a Jewish menorah, some bread and wine, and fruit and flowers.

While this is going on, have four people read the script or listen to the audio of the conversation of a family building their Shelter in the time when the Israelites had just settled in the promised land and their desert wandering was over.

Bible talk

With: several people ready with personal stories; items or props to add to the shelter

Summarise the main themes as shown below from the Festival of Shelters being explored in the service. Invite the congregation to suggest examples of how we do each of these three things as Christians today. You could illustrate each theme by attaching appropriate items to the shelter.

Rejoice (Leviticus 23:40)
This does not mean just being happy, but 'rejoicing before the Lord your God' – being happy with and because of God. Recap how this has already been done in the service. Add some celebratory items to the Shelter, such as balloons or tinsel.

Remember (verses 42–43)
The shelters were to be reminders of the time the Israelites were in the desert moving from place to place. It might seem more like something to forget. But God wanted them to remember where they had begun – in the desert. (Place a large tray heaped with sand inside the shelter if you are using **Prayers of intercession**.) We too remember beginning steps in our journey with God.

Some people today have brought things which

remind them of a time when they learned about depending on God. Invite these people forward and ask each one to tell everyone about that time in just one or two sentences and then to place the object in or on the shelter. Examples could include when a friend or family member was ill or in danger; when church finances hit a crisis; during World War 2; a redundancy; being bullied at school.

Rely (verses 42–43)
Why should the people remember the time in the desert at harvest festival? When we are comfortable it is easy to give God a lower place in our lives. In the desert the Israelites had to learn that they depended on God for everything they needed to live. We too need to remember that we rely on God for everything. At harvest, we especially remember that we rely on him for our food and material needs. Add appropriate items to the shelter, such as some fruit or a cross.

Prayer of confession
With: a piece of damaged fruit

Show a piece of fruit which is damaged and unattractive to eat. Say: as we celebrate what God has given, we also need to say sorry to him for the times we have spoiled his creation by using it wrongly.

Lead this prayer of confession, with everyone saying the words in bold:

God our Father, we are sorry for the times when we have been careless with your gifts or acted ungratefully.
Forgive us, Father, and make us grateful.

We enjoy the fruits of the harvest, but sometimes forget that it is you who has given them to us.
Forgive us, Father, and make us grateful.

We are never starving and our stomachs are satisfied, but we ignore the cry of the hungry.
Forgive us, Father, and make us grateful.

We are thoughtless, and do not care enough for your world.
Forgive us, Father, and make us grateful.

We frantically make sure that we are short of nothing, as if there were no God and no heaven.
Forgive us, Father, and make us grateful.
Following the confession, read these words from

Psalm 103:8–12 (CEV):

> The LORD is merciful!
> He is kind and patient, and his love never fails.
> The LORD won't always be angry and point out our sins;
> he doesn't punish us as our sins deserve.
> How great is God's love for all who worship him?
> Greater than the distance between heaven and earth!
> How far has the LORD taken our sins from us?
> Farther than the distance from east to west!

Prayer activity
With: 'flags' made by doubling a self-adhesive address label around one end of a cocktail stick; pens or pencils; sand tray

Give each person two simple 'flags'. Invite them to draw or write on one flag any situation or person they want to pray for today. On the other, invite them to write their own name or draw themselves.

Remind everyone that the shelter is a reminder of the Israelites learning that they had to depend on God – to trust him whatever the situation. Invite everyone to bring their flags and stick them in the sand tray in the shelter as a way of bringing those situations to God and expressing our own dependence on him.

An alternative **Prayers of intercession** (AASA4.Harvest_3) is available online.

Ending the service
With: bowls of fresh or dried fruit pieces

Pass the fruit around and invite everyone to take some, to hold it but not eat it – yet. When everyone has been served, remind them of the themes of remembering and rejoicing that have come together during your 'festival to remember'. Repeat the praise shout from **Beginning the service**.

Eat the fruit and let the smell, the texture and the taste remind you of the greatness of the God who made it all!

Helpful extras

Music and song ideas

'All creatures of our God and king' *SOF* 645
'All things bright and beautiful' *ks* 8
'Bring in the harvest' *ks* 427
'Gives! Gives! Gives!' *ks* 67
'Harvest time' *ks* 95
'It takes an almighty hand' *ks* 176
'Let everything that has breath' *ks* 623
'Now thank we all our God' *SOF* 405
'The earth is the Lord's' *SOF* 528
'We plough the fields and scatter' *SOF* 585
'Who put the colours in the rainbow?' *ks* 386

Listen to John Rutter's delicate arrangement of 'For the beauty of the earth' or 'All things bright and beautiful' (*The Ultimate Collection*, Universal Classics; ASIN B001GYNIEY; also available as MP3 downloads).

Game

With: fruit from around the world, for tasting

If appropriate, comment on the fruit (of all kinds) which are part of the decorations and harvest gifts. In Israel, the Festival of Shelters follows after the harvesting of fruit through the summer – grapes, olives, dates and figs. Around the world, people enjoy many different fruits at harvest time.

Challenge members of the congregation to identify different fruits from around the world by taste alone. (Ask your volunteers to close their eyes.) The taste challenge could include the citron fruit – which plays an important part in the Jewish celebrations of 'Sukkot' – as the 'best fruit' of Leviticus 23:40.

This could be organised as a quiz between two teams or the two sides of the church. Comment again on the variety of wonderful fruit that we enjoy – that God has given us – and the other ways in which we use the word 'fruit' – for all the good things that God makes us able to produce. (Remember to follow hygiene guidelines and check for allergies.)

Notes and comments

With many thanks to the Diocese of Liverpool and CPAS for their generous permission to use and adapt freely many of the original ideas in this service. For more details visit www.givingingrace.org

In 2011AD, which is the Jewish year 5772, 'Sukkot' begins at sunset on October 12 and ends at nightfall on October 19. For more online information about 'Sukkot' visit www.jewfaq.org (an encyclopaedia of Orthodox Judaism); or search Wikipedia.org for 'Sukkot' and 'Sukkah'.

During the joyful celebration of the Festival of Shelters, the whole 'Hallel' is said. This is a block of six psalms (113–118), 85 verses in total, about eight minutes of reading aloud (or longer, with multiple readers)! Don't be put off by the length of the reading. If you are eager, others will catch your enthusiasm and it is an opportunity for everyone to contribute something to the service, building up others. A 'script' for the 'Hallel' (AASA4.Harvest_4) is available, using the CEV.

Provide materials for people to make the equivalent of a lulav (a streamer traditionally made by tying together a palm branch, two willow branches and three myrtle branches) to carry around the church today, as the shelter is being constructed or for a procession around the building. Details of this tradition and suggestions for making one are available (AASA4. Harvest_5). This activity would be especially valuable to include younger children.

Ideas for making the most of your harvest festival (AASA4.Harvest_6) are available, as are 'take home' sheets for all ages that extend this service into a Week of Harvest (AASA4. Harvest_7).

Bible resources

These are all Scripture Union storybooks that you can use to bring Bible stories alive in an all-age service. *The Big Bible Storybook* is especially suitable for under fives and is available as a book and an audio book.

The Strong Tower
978 1 84427 122 1
£7.99

10 Must Know Stories
978 1 84427 326 3
£3.99

Must Know Stories
978 1 84427 320 1
£7.99

The Big Bible Storybook Timeline
978 1 84427 3614
£11.99

The Big Bible Storybook
(hardback)
978 1 84427 228 0
£12.99

The Big Bible Storybook
(audio book)
978 1 84427 379 9
£19.99

Make sure that everyone knows what Bible reading guides are available, to equip people to meet with God regularly as they read the Bible. Make a special effort to encourage families to read the Bible together.

Encourage people to visit www.wordlive.org, Scripture Union's online Bible reading site.

Prices are correct at the time of going to print. All are available from good Christian bookshops or Scripture Union Mail Order or online – www.scriptureunion.org.uk/shop

All-age resources

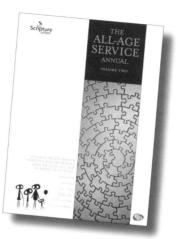

All-age Service Annual volume 1
978 1 84427 316 4
All-age Service Annual volume 2
978 1 84427 341 6

Take the stress out of the planning for your monthly all-age service with 15 complete and creative all-age service outlines. Can be used in conjunction with the *Light* syllabus. Additional material available as downloads.

All-age Service Annual 3
978 1 84427 381 2

Includes 15 service outlines plus 52 sets of all-age service starters outlines and starters. Can be used in conjunction with the *Light* syllabus. Additional material available as downloads.

All-age Lectionary Services Year A
978 1 84427 504 5

The services in the first year of Light for the Lectionary have been significantly revised or new material has been written to ensure that all-age worship leaders have this easy-to-use toolbox which enables them to lead all-age services throughout the Lectionary Year A. Free taster also available.

Top Tips on All-age worship
978 1 84427 125 0

An inspirational look at why all-age worship is not only desirable but doable in your church! Explore some of the features of an all-age church and think about the different components of a worship service and how to use them. Plus practical pointers on issues such as planning, leadership and getting creative.